The Protocol School of Washington®

TEA &
ETIQUETTE

First paperback edition 2000
Copyright © 1998 by Dorothea Johnson

Published by Capital Books Inc.
22883 Quicksilver Drive
Sterling, Virginia 20166

ATTENTION: ORGANIZATIONS
Capital Books are available at quantity dis-
counts with bulk purchase for educational,
business, or sales promotional use. For
information, please write to: Special Sales
Department, Capital Books, P.O. Box 605,
Herndon, Virginia 20172-0605 or call
1-800-758-3756.

Library of Congress
Cataloging-in-Publication Data
    Johnson, Dorothea.
    Tea & Etiquette: Taking Tea for Business
    and Pleasure / by Dorothea Johnson; with
    an introduction by James Norwood Pratt.
    p. cm.
    ISBN 1-892123-35-5
    1. Afternoon teas—United States.
    2. Table etiquette—United States. I. Title.
    TX736.J64 1998
    641.5'3—dc21
    98-41075 CIP

Cover and illustrations by Antonia Walker
Book design by Caroline Brock

Printed in the United States

The Protocol School of Washington®

TEA &
ETIQUETTE

Taking Tea for Business and Pleasure

by

Dorothea Johnson

With an introduction by
James Norwood Pratt

CAPITAL BOOKS INC.
WASHINGTON D.C.

Also by Dorothea Johnson

Entertaining and Etiquette for Today (Acropolis, 1979)

The Little Book of Etiquette (Running Press, 1997)

For my family

Bebe, Liv, Ann, Ted, Julia, Tom, Jim, and Heather

Acknowledgments

*T*his book is more than a recent venture into the world of tea. It is the result of a lifetime of learning, a lifetime blessed with knowing many people who have contributed to my learning process and to this book.

For those who stand beside me and never fail to add their support and considerable talents, I thank Deborah Onesty, Caroline Becker, Gillian French, Ann Noyes, and Robert Hickey.

I shall be eternally grateful to my dear friend, James Norwood Pratt, for writing, in his elegant and witty style, the introduction to this book. Norwood is, in the truest spirit, a generous and patient tutor in the mysteries of tea.

John Harney, master tea blender, told me in no uncertain terms, "Dorothea, you must serve a polite cup of tea with your book!" After our telephone conversation, I tossed about several tea-related words and finally chose "Civilitea," because to me tea makes us feel more civilized.

"Civilitea" complements this book and The Protocol School of Washington®'s Tea & Etiquette programs. Norwood Pratt and Michael Harney teamed up to blend an excellent, "refreshingly polite" black tea. "Civilitea" is blended exclusively for The Protocol School of Washington® by Harney & Sons Fine Teas.

Since November 1991, The Ritz-Carlton, Tysons Corner, family has hosted The Protocol School of Washington®'s functions in the highest professional manner.

For sharing their delicious recipes, I thank the following: Executive Chef Jacques Sorci of The Ritz-Carlton, Tysons Corner; Shelley and Bruce Richardson, owners of Elmwood Inn, Perryville, Kentucky; Kay Snipes and Terri Eager, owners of Magnolia & Ivy tearooms, Plains, Georgia; and Dr. Anil Sanghera, India and Baltimore, Maryland.

I also acknowledge, with respect and admiration, the men and women who are teaching The Protocol School of Washington®'s curriculum. Through teaching the principles of etiquette, they are promoting values intrinsic to a civil society.

For her help and dedication, I thank my publisher, Kathleen Hughes.

Contents

Preface

*T*oday, afternoon tea is one of the fastest-growing trends in America, and it is riding a wave of popularity around the world. There is an attractive, timeless quality about going to tea; and hotels, country inns, museums, and tearooms are competing to re-create the atmosphere of a bygone era. No matter where it occurs, there is a calming, eternal charm about the whole affair that is irresistible. Tea beckons us to enjoy quality time with friends and loved ones, and especially to rediscover the art of relaxed conversation.

Afternoon tea conjures up feelings of elegance and gentility. It is, after all, synonymous with civility and blessed with the endearing quality of being just a touch highbrow. The customs and courtesies associated with this most civilized ceremony, however, are disquieting to the uninitiated. Fear of committing "tea faux pas" is on the upturn, as tea is now serving not only a social function, but a professional one as well—an alternative to the business lunch or dinner. This has created an unprecedented demand for learning the essentials of tea etiquette as executives meet in hotel lounges to discuss business over a cup of tea.

While there is infinite pleasure in taking tea, it is also cloaked with a system of rules designed, I believe, to civilize and calm our more primitive side. To me, the ritualized exchange of courtesies at a tea gathering illustrates, in microcosm, the central role of etiquette in human life. At tea, as in any other interaction, we are not free to act merely as we please; but we must act with mutual consideration, as befits our interdependence. Sharing tea provides us with a perfect opportunity to express this truth in action. Observing courtesies, that is, sympathetic coordination, allows host and guest to achieve a harmony that transcends their respective roles. This attitude of considerate harmony can extend also to the inanimate utensils we use and to the very tea itself. In this way, the peace and poetry of life that we all seek can be found reflected in a simple cup of tea.

This book includes elements of both social and business tea etiquette, since you may be called upon to be host or guest at either as afternoon tea becomes an ever-popular way to entertain. The book begins with some of the fascinating history and custom that surround the tea ceremony to give you an understanding of its importance worldwide. You will find a brief description of many teas and the equipment that has been developed for serving tea so that you may sample its infinite variety. My tea-loving friends have also contributed some of their favorite recipes to accompany this most pleasant of dining times with friends or business associates.

While I have made every effort not to tell you more than you really want to know, I have also made every effort to provide contemporary information that will give you the heart of grace to enjoy yourself at tea and to interact with kindness and respect to those around you.

Dorothea Johnson, Director
The Protocol School
of Washington®
1998

Introduction

By James Norwood Pratt

*I*f someone as formidable as Lady Bracknell of Oscar Wilde's *The Importance of Being Earnest* were to invite me to tea, I'd know exactly what to do: Call Dorothea Johnson! Not even the loftiest and most English ceremony of afternoon tea daunts Dorothea. By the time she got through with me, I could not be intimidated by even so imposing a grande dame as Her Ladyship. In fact, I'd be prepared to enjoy her company as well as her tea and myself into the bargain.

A leading American "mannerist," Dorothea has been helping men, women, and children learn manners since 1957. She prepares her students to enjoy life to the fullest by making them secure in life's fundamental social graces. It takes a very little bit of extra poise and understanding to produce a vastly different impression on others—and vastly greater pleasure for all.

It is a particularly blessed event to herald Dorothea Johnson's work on the etiquette of tea, for this is an arena where her coaching will prove invaluable. In the aftermath of the Boston Tea Party, Americans were born with a prenatal disinclination for tea. Today, with the encouragement of trendsetters like Dorothea, we are rediscovering what a healthful habit and adjunct to social joy tea can be. But are we sure we know what we're doing?

The drinking of tea, like the making of it, calls for a certain amount of ceremony or ritual. The steps in the ritual of tea making follow a prescribed order because they MUST: You cannot pour the tea until it has steeped; you cannot steep the tea until you have heated the water; et cetera. In drinking tea, the ceremony to be observed may seem less logical, perhaps, but it is no less necessary. This is because tea is pre-eminently a social beverage, and any social situation calls for manners. In fact, the ceremonies of teatime can raise our manners to the pinnacle of refinement.

We cannot refine what we have not got, however.

A teatime ritual of some sort has evolved in every culture and in every time where tea has played a role. While the Japanese tea ceremony or the use of the samovar may be of passing interest, it is the Black Tea Ceremony as developed in England that we encounter with increasing frequency in our social and business life today. This is the focus of Dorothea's book, and we will all be just that much more civilized for learning what she has to teach us.

One reason tea makes us feel good is because of its physical effects. The caffeine it contains banishes fatigue and lifts our spirits without coffee's jolt or letdown, at the same time its healthful polyphenols act to calm us. Tea is the only substance known that both stimulates and soothes. But the sense of genial well-being tea imparts comes in large measure, I believe, from the tea ceremony itself. It is an exchange of simple courtesies and the sharing of a simple pleasure that induces a pleasant harmony not otherwise obtainable. Just as it is a ceremony which always calls for using beautiful things—silver, porcelain, linens, et cetera—to enhance it, so also it always allows our most beautiful comportment. All this, taken together, is why tea is one of those things that always make us feel a little more civilized, and all this is what Dorothea Johnson teaches.

"Virtue gone to seed" is what Emerson called courtesy, as if to prove great minds can also have blind spots. He might have been corrected—tactfully, one feels sure—by his great contemporary Goethe, who justly observed: "There is no external sign of courtesy without a deep ethical cause." The author of this book is on the side of Goethe, not Emerson. If the world we inhabit is by ever so little more thoughtful and more mannerly, and, if we are more at home in it, this is in no small measure thanks to the effects of tea and to teachers like Dorothea Johnson.

James Norwood Pratt
San Francisco, California
1998

Part I: Tea Tantalizers

Chapter One

Tea–Past and Present

*Tea tempers the spirits
and harmonizes the
mind, dispels lassitude
and relieves fatigue,
awakens thought and
prevents drowsiness,
lightens or refreshes
the body, and clears
the perceptive faculties.*

LU YU
EIGHTH-CENTURY
CHINESE POET

*L*egends abound about the discovery of tea with the origins of the beverage shrouded in Oriental folklore. My favorite legend credits the Chinese Emperor Shen Nung, who discovered that the boiling of water made it safe to drink. One day, almost five thousand years ago, as the emperor was waiting for his pot to boil, leaves from a bush nearby fell into the hot water. The emperor drank the liquid and found it tasty, refreshing, and relaxing.

The wild plant was *Camellia sinensis*, which can grow to approximately 15 feet. The China plant is very hardy and can withstand extreme cold temperature. The leaves are approximately two inches long.

Camellia assamica is considered a tree and can grow up to 65 feet if not reduced to the plucking level of about 4 feet. The leaf is six times as large as the *sinensis* leaf.

The *Camellia assamica* subspecies *lasiocalyx* is also a tree that grows to about 15 feet. The leaf size is intermediate between *sinensis* and *assamica*.

Black, oolong, green, white, and Puerh are different types of tea that are all produced by different methods of processing the leaf from the same plant, *Camellia sinensis*. Different regions, climate, soil, and subvariety of the plant determine the variations in flavor and appearance among teas of the same type. Keemun from China, Darjeeling from India, and Ceylon from Sri Lanka are all black teas, for example, but they look and taste very different. White and Puerh teas are native to China and are seldom sold in this country.

Today, India and Sri Lanka supply more than half of the world's tea. Other major tea growers are China, Japan, Indonesia, Kenya, and Taiwan. Turkey, Iran, Brazil, Russia, Mozambique, Uganda, Malawi, Bangladesh, Tanzania, Zaire, Vietnam, and Argentina also grow the *Camellia sinensis* plant commercially.

South Carolina and Hawaii are the only locations in the United States where tea estates currently grow, process, and market a black tea.

The English and Tea

By the 1650s, coffeehouses were an established part of London life. These houses were the only places selling tea to drink. Loose tea was stocked by apothecaries for medicinal purposes. Some of the brand names are still in existence in

If you are cold, tea will warm you. If you are heated, it will cool you. If you are depressed, it will cheer you. If you are excited, it will calm you.

WILLIAM EWART
GLADSTONE
(1809–1898)

England today. "Typhoo" was thought to be the
Chinese word for doctor. "PG Tips" stood for Pre-
Gestive Tips. "99 Tea" was known as doctors' or
prescription tea.

Thomas Garway, a general merchant, was
the first to advertise tea for sale at his
"Cophee-House, in Sweeting's Rents by the
Royal Exchange." His announcement in a
September 23–30, 1658, weekly London news-
paper proclaimed, "The excellent and by all
physitans approved China drink, called by the
Chineans Tcha, by other nations Tay, alias Tee."
Two years later in 1660, he published a lengthy
pamphlet entitled, "An Exact Description of the
Growth, Quality and Vertues of the Leaf Tee,"
which claimed that tea would cure almost any
known ailment and

> *. . . maketh the Body active and lusty*
> *. . . helpeth the Head-ache, giddiness*
> *and heaviness thereof . . . taketh away*
> *the difficulty of breathing, opening*
> *Obstructions . . . is good against*
> *Liptitude, Distillations, and cleareth*
> *the Sight . . . it vanquisheth heavy*
> *Dreams, easeth the Brain and*
> *strengtheneth the Memory, it over-*
> *cometh superfluous Sleep, and*
> *prevents Sleepiness in general . . . it is*
> *good for Cold, Dropsies and Scurveys*
> *and expelleth Infection.*

Samuel Pepys recorded in his diary for September 25, 1660, that in the middle of a very busy day he "did send for a cupp of tee (a China drink) of which I had never drank before." His entry for June 28, 1667, confirms that tea was still looked upon as a medicine as well as a refreshing beverage. He wrote that he arrived "home and found my wife making of tee, a drink Mr. Pelling, the potticary, tells her is good for her cold and defluxions."

Samuel Johnson (1709–1784), the famous lexicographer, described himself in *The Literary Magazine* as:

> *A hardened and shameless tea-drinker, who has, for twenty years diluted his meals with only the infusion of this fascinating plant; whose kettle has scarcely time to cool; who with tea muses the evening, with tea solaces the midnight, and with tea welcomes the morning.*

James Boswell's *Life of Johnson* contains many references to tea drinking, such as:

> *It was perfectly normal for him to drink sixteen cups in very quick succession, and I suppose no person ever enjoyed with more relish the infusion of that fragrant leaf than did Johnson.*

In 1678, the East India Company began to import tea commercially. It was an expensive luxury that only the wealthy could afford. At first, mistakes were made by cooks and others in the preparation of tea. One gentleman had it served up as greens for his table; the water in which the leaves were boiled was thrown away.

In the seventeenth and eighteenth centuries, many serious-minded Britons opposed the introduction of tea. In 1678, Henry Saville denounced tea drinking as "a filthy custom, causing men to lose their stature and comeliness and women their beauty through the use of tea."

John Wesley campaigned against the drink, professing that it caused "some symptoms of a Paralytick disorder."

Jonas Hanway wrote in his *Essay on Tea,* that it was "robbing the people of their health and the nation of its wealth."

In 1759, Dick Wormward warned the citizens: "That beauty and virtue of women will soon be destroyed by the use of tea."

Even as late as 1830 William Cobbett, in his *Advice to Young Men and Women,* said:

> *Free yourself from the slavery of tea and coffee . . . can any good labourer look back upon the last thirty years of his life without cursing the day on which tea was introduced into England?!*

He also stated that:

> *Tea is an enfeebler of the frame, an engenderer of effeminacy and laziness, a debaucher of youth and a maker of misery for old age.*

The Boston Tea Party

Taxing tea in the American colonies angered the people to such an extent that on December 16, 1773, fifty men disguised as Indians and armed with hatchets and pistols attacked the three tea ships anchored at Boston. They broke open and dumped into the harbor 342 chests of tea. This was only the most famous of the ten or twelve vigilante demonstrations, or "tea parties," that occurred throughout the American colonies. From having been the favorite American drink, tea became the symbol of oppression, and people started to drink coffee instead.

Chapter Two

Tea Tales—Some of My Favorite Teatimes

*T*he aim of taking tea is to share goodwill, which has led me over the years to spend many happy hours over tea with friends and colleagues. Many of these teas have been purely social; others have led to important business contracts or contacts. All have provided time for reflection, quiet conversation, and, of course, excitement—an important element of life.

For seasoned tea drinkers and those new to these pleasantries, I have described a few of my memorable teatimes. These teatimes were filled with pleasures, as well as perils, all of which make the cup that cheers an energizing ritual.

Newport, Rhode Island

Newport was a glorious place to live during the late 1960s, with formal entertaining *de rigueur* and afternoon tea a daily happening. Each setting was more beautiful and formal than the previous one.

Sunday high tea at the Weilers' in their pink Bermuda-style home on Cliff Walk was always a special treat. Rena Weiler was a du Pont and the niece of Charles Schwab, the financier. Admiral Weiler, long retired from the Navy, was her seventh and last husband. Both Weilers were in their late seventies, but their age didn't keep them from being great party givers and goers.

High tea at the Weilers' was an abundant, beautifully presented buffet supper, and while tea was served during the social hour and with dessert, it was not as popular as some of the more potent beverages. This, of course, never daunted Rena. At the end of high tea, around eight o'clock, her butler handed each guest tea in a disposable cup as they walked out the door. Rena claimed it was an antidote to "those other beverages" and made driving safer.

One afternoon tea that I particularly remember was the one to which Jackie Onassis's mother, Mrs. Hugh Auchincloss, invited members of the Officers' Wives Club. Hammersmith Farm was a sprawling, twenty-eight-room estate on eighty-three acres, filled with lovely antiques which bespoke of understated elegance. The oriental carpets were faded to a warm hue with a few worn spots, all of which added to the beauty and charm of the place. The sofas and chairs were covered in exquisite muted silks.

I sat motionless in a chair, my eyes drinking in the surrounding lived-in elegance. Both armrests on the chair were so frayed I was afraid to touch either one and purposely sat with my arms close to my body, as all Southern ladies are taught to do, and held my teacup waist level as I sipped.

Fearing melancholy, I went to refill my teacup and returned to find "my chair" had been commandeered by a woman who was busily picking at the threads on the left armrest. How dare she touch those wonderfully worn silk threads! I could only imagine the times Jackie had sat in that chair, and who knows the other famous people, including President Kennedy. After about five minutes, the "thread picker" rose from the chair as her left hand found her jacket pocket. At last, I could reclaim "my chair" and continue to savor this room; but as I sat down I saw that a large patch of the fabric had been picked and pulled from the left armrest. Horrified that someone would think I had done this terrible thing, I sprang from the chair, distanced myself from it, and remained standing for the duration of "Tea at Hammersmith Farm."

My favorite "Newport Teas" were hosted by Hope Johnston, the beautiful blonde wife of the admiral who commanded the Navy base. Schooled in Europe, Hope was an elegant, aristocratic woman who knew more about entertaining than anyone I had met. I liked to observe how she did things, because each occasion was a learning experience. Of course, it was enormously helpful to her that she had a first-rate staff at hand.

At one such tea, I had properly gone through the receiving line and executed the obligatory greetings to the other ladies when Hope beckoned to me. I hastened to her side as she commanded, "Dorothea, keep an eye on the finger sandwiches; one of the stewards is ill." Well, I was absolutely flattered and honored to police those finger sandwiches. The tray looked full and beautifully arranged, and I walked a few steps away to get a cup of tea only to return and find the tray practically empty, yet no one had been near this area of the table. Puzzled, I went to the kitchen for replacements, only to have this supply vanish within minutes.

Back to the kitchen I went, but this time I decided to keep my eyes on the filled tray. Very shortly, I spotted a hand emerging from under the skirted table, groping for the sandwich tray. I bent down and carefully lifted the long tablecloth to find the Johnston's twelve-year-old son, Means III, under the table hosting his own party with Mr. Dog, the schnauzer, as guest of honor. He politely greeted me with, "Oh hello, Mrs. Johnson. It's very nice to see you."

Republic of China

As the guest of a prominent Chinese business owner, I dined in many restaurants in Taiwan that were not frequented by tourists. One particular restaurant stands out vividly in my memory because my host said, "Anna Chennault always goes there; it is the best." Anna Chennault is the widow of the famous World War II Flying Tigers hero, General Claire Chennault. She still resides in her magnificent penthouse at The Watergate in Washington, D.C.

Several of the restaurant staff approached our table and bowed, and never turned their backs to us as they served or when they exited the room. A covered cup was placed first in front of me, then the other two Americans, and lastly our host. Fearing the unknown, I hesitated to touch the cup and, timidly whispered to my host, "Please explain."

"Lift the lid and look inside and see the tea," he coaxed. I saw leaves floating in tea and wondered how I could drink without swallowing most of them. He quickly showed us how to use the lid to hold back the leaves as we drank the tea.

As one constantly in pursuit of new dining experiences, this was, I thought, a heady venture. The food was the best, just as our host had promised.

Washington, D.C.

I met Mrs. Frederick Chien, wife of the ambassador to the United States from the Republic of China, at a social event. During our conversation, I relayed my covered teacup experiences, which seemed to please her. Within a few days, I received an engraved dinner invitation to Twin Oaks, the ambassador's residence, along with a personal note telling me that tea would be served just as I had enjoyed it in Taiwan.

The reader should be aware that this took place before former President Jimmy Carter extended formal diplomatic recognition to the People's Republic of China on the mainland in 1979. Part of the deal was to "derecognize" the Republic of China on Taiwan in just about every category except trade.

There were several Americans at the dinner, and I persuaded Mrs. Chien to demonstrate how to properly drink from the covered cup. She did, and it was a huge hit! On each visit during the following years we always drank from a covered cup, called the *gaiwan*.

Twenty years later, I met the incredibly urbane James Norwood Pratt, who is recognized as America's leading tea expert. Norwood is directly responsible for this country's new found knowledge and passion for tea.

I was elated when he agreed to come on board as The Protocol School of Washington®'s tea expert. As our tea guru, his first command was, "Get me three dozen *gaiwans!* I will need them to properly demonstrate their usage."

"Right away, Master Pratt, just tell me where," I replied. Norwood's tea tutorings are always a highlight at our tea trainings. This man has more admirers, including *moi,* than anyone I know.

Tea in the Dining Room

I was invited to a Sunday afternoon tea by the charming wife of a German diplomat. They had rented a lovely old house in Georgetown and filled it with European and American antiques.

The dining room table, in this case, was treated as a large tea table; no places were set and each guest took a seat at the table, a custom that is followed in many European countries. The tea tray was placed at one end of the table, where the hostess sat; the food, the little plates, and napkins were in the middle.

As we sat enjoying each others' company, the beauty of the room, the tea, and food, the man and woman across the table appeared to be quite angry and exchanged rather heated words. I heard her say, "Well, how dare you!" And he replied, "How dare I what?" followed by her, "If you do it once more I shall tell my husband." He replied, "How can I do it once more when I have not done it at all?"

I was astounded at such behavior. People simply don't fight at teas. They fight at bars, but not in someone's elegant Georgetown dining room during afternoon tea.

Just when the argument reached a fever pitch, just when I expected her to empty her teacup in his face, our host rose, walked around the table, stood between the feuding pair, and said in a most diplomatic way, "Excuse me, please," as he dropped to his knees, lifted the tablecloth and pulled his dog, Fritz, a weimaraner, from under the table. Fritz had apparently been rubbing his nose against the woman's knees, begging for food no doubt, while she was convinced the man seated next to her was making passes under the table. We all had a good laugh and begged our hosts to let us borrow dear Fritz to liven up our parties. Alas, Fritz was not available as party entertainment.

McLean, Virginia

A client, the CEO of a high-tech firm, called me and said, "Dorothea, I have been invited to tea by this Brit, and I think I need some help. My wife said, 'Be sure to hold out your pinkie when you pick up the teacup.'"

I gently told him, "Be sure you don't hold out your pinkie. Now with that settled, tell me about the times you have drunk tea."

He answered, "When I was a little boy and had a cold, my grandmother always gave me tea and honey. What I really need is to drink tea, talk business, and not look like a clod."

We set a date for him to join me at my office for a "tea tutorial." He was a very attentive pupil as we practiced the rudiments of taking tea, and he never raised his little finger.

As my tutoring was drawing to an end, I extracted two promises from him. Promise number one: Drink tea each afternoon, instead of coffee. After all, he needed the practice. I had demonstrated how to make a pot of tea and even supplied him with a tin of my favorite Darjeeling and a tea filter. Promise number two: Call and debrief me the day after the tea date, which was to take place five days later.

Right on schedule, he called, and his voice told me everything had gone well. "I felt comfortable from start to finish while the other two Americans appeared quite awkward during the eating part and didn't seem to relax until near the end; I felt cool and confident throughout tea."

The soul of politeness is not a question of rules but of tranquility, humility, and simplicity. And in the taking of tea it finds perhaps its most perfect expression.

The Japanese Tea Ceremony

I have had the pleasure and honor of attending tea ceremonies both in Japan and at the Embassy of Japan in Washington, D.C. My good friend James Norwood Pratt expressed my reaction perfectly in his marvelous book, *The Tea Lover's Treasury*, when he wrote: "Life is too short to attend enough Japanese tea ceremonies to form an intelligent opinion of them."

While it may be impossible for the casual onlooker to understand what she or he is witnessing, the Japanese Tea Ceremony undeniably gives you something to think about.

Practitioners and students not only in Japan but around the world devote lifetimes to *cha-no-yu* or "hot water for tea"—beyond doubt the most ritualized way of taking tea ever practiced. But becoming an expert at performing this ritual is not the point. Students of the "Way of Tea" eventually realize that the formalities and rules are not meant as an end in themselves. They are intended to express, through the serving and receiving of a cup of tea, a certain understanding of life itself.

It is, I believe, just as James Norwood Pratt has written: "The Japanese cult of the tea ceremony aims beyond beauty, whether of objects or of comportment, at glimpses of the Ultimate."

I am not a student of the Japanese Tea Ceremony, but it has helped me understand that etiquette ultimately depends upon a state of mind. The soul of politeness is not a question of rules but of tranquility, humility, and simplicity. And in the taking of tea it finds perhaps its most perfect expression.

Teaism is a cult founded on the adoration of the beautiful among the sordid facts of everyday existence. It inculcates purity and harmony, the mystery of mutual charity, the romanticism of the social order.

OKAKURA KAKUZO
BOOK OF TEA

Osaka, Japan

I was fortunate to have a friend who had lived in Japan for almost two years when I arrived there for a two-month stay. She patiently explained the rituals of the tea ceremony and even performed her modified, albeit Americanized version, all of which I found enormously fascinating.

Within days, an invitation arrived to participate in a tea ceremony. We called upon our hostess three days before the tea to accept and to express our gratitude.

The day of the tea, we gathered with another guest in the waiting room twenty minutes before the time stated on the invitation. The seating order was established then with the honor bestowed on the mother of a German diplomat. This procedure works two ways: The seating order is often predetermined, or it is decided after the guests arrive, beginning with the eldest or highest ranking and ending with someone well versed in the ceremony. I felt very fortunate: The well-versed someone was my friend.

The first part of the ceremony began when the hostess entered, bowed silently, and we bowed in return. Then the hostess left the room. From this moment forward, everything that happened was rigidly set. We arranged ourselves in the prescribed order and changed into clean socks. Then we left all of our belongings in the waiting room and took the path through the garden to the teahouse, or *sukiya*.

Teahouses vary in size, although the ones I saw in Japan were approximately nine feet square. Entrance to the *sukiya* was through a low, small door. The intent is to humble high and low alike.

After cleansing our hands in basins, we crawled one at a time through the door to the tearoom. Once inside, it was our duty to turn and rearrange our shoes and move them out of the way.

Inside the tearoom, we went to the *tokonoma*, an alcove containing a scroll, and bowed again. After the last person had entered, we seated ourselves, in the predetermined order, on rice mats called *tatami* and talked quietly among ourselves. We praised the garden, the *tokonoma,* and the fragrance of the incense.

The hostess entered, personally greeted each guest, and then lighted incense in the charcoal. The honored guest then requested, on behalf of the others, that we be permitted to admire the incense case, which is always an heirloom of the family.

A light meal of many small courses followed. One was expected to always say,
"O-saki ni," anytime one did anything before
another guest.

At the end of the meal, we retired to the
garden to relax, listen to the wind, and chat
quietly among ourselves. During this time, our
hostess was busy preparing the tea utensils, tidy-
ing the room, and exchanging the scroll for a
flower arrangement.

A hostess may let her guests know she is
ready for them by sounding a gong or appearing
and bowing silently. Our hostess chose to bow.

We re-entered the *sukiya* and admired the
flower arrangement. Next we looked at the kettle,
the fire, and the tea caddy before taking our seats
on the *tatami*.

Our hostess returned and prepared a thick
tea called *koicha*. This thick tea was passed from
guest to guest in one big tea bowl. The etiquette of
drinking in this manner required that I place the
silk cloth on my left palm, then carefully set the
bowl on the cloth and steady it with my right
hand. Then with a nod and an "O-saki ni" to the
next guest, I turned the bowl twice clockwise so
that the design was facing away.

After taking three-and-a-half sips, I put the bowl down, picked up my little cloth, and wiped the edge of the bowl from which I drank. Then I turned it with the design facing me again and passed it to the guest on my right.

After each guest drank from the bowl, it was returned to the hostess, who passed it back to us to examine. She told us the history of the bowl. Our duty as guests was to inquire about and examine carefully every utensil used in the tea preparation. To remain silent would have been offensive.

Then a thin tea called *usucha* was served with small cakes. The overall feeling was far more relaxed than at any other time. Each of us was served tea, one at a time, in separate bowls. The only firm etiquette in drinking this tea was to wipe the edge of the bowl I drank from with my thumb and index finger, and then wipe those on my napkin.

The utensils were put away with care and reverence. We expressed our gratitude, and the tea ceremony was over. More than four hours had slipped by since our hostess first bowed to us in the waiting room. It barely seemed like an hour, and we marveled at how totally relaxed and at peace we felt.

Each of us sent our hostess a thank-you note, which was delivered by messenger, not the mail. An alternative would have been to visit our hostess and offer thanks in person. Both methods were considered quite proper.

While this particular tea ceremony is a common one, it is not the only style of tea ceremony offered. However, it is typical of the tea ceremonies I participated in while in Japan. The length of time may vary as witnessed at several tea ceremonies in the Washington, D.C., area. At all of the teas, hosted by women from the Embassy of Japan, the way one conducted oneself was important. We watched each other closely to make sure we were doing the right thing, and we made every effort to appreciate the tranquility and beauty of this most ritualized way of taking tea.

Tea Dances

My first encounter with the tea dance occurred in the early 1950s at The Cavalier Beach Club in Virginia Beach, Virginia. During the summer season, there was a dance every day of the week. This was the place to go, see, and be seen. The Beach Club, as it was known, was quite exclusive, with a clientele of members, guests of members, and guests of The Cavalier Hotel.

A doorman opened the closely guarded entrance, and one had to present a membership card to the receptionist, who checked it against her list. Inside the club, one walked down a corridor leading to a huge, open outdoor area overlooking the Atlantic Ocean. Tables and chairs crowded the borders of the dance floor on three outdoor areas while the orchestra occupied the center of the fourth enclosed area, with additional tables and chairs filling the remaining space.

The tea dances began at four o'clock, and the place was jumping by 4:30. These were friendly gatherings, where everyone had a wonderful time dancing to the orchestra and visiting at various tables. Women dressed in their loveliest tea dresses, the men wore suits and ties, and children dressed like young ladies and gentlemen. Girls danced with fathers and grandfathers, while boys danced with mothers and grandmothers. And the boys and girls even danced with each other. Time seemed to fly by until around 6:00, when people started drifting out to go to dinner or perhaps a party at someone's home.

Today, afternoon tea dances and tango teas are becoming very popular again as hotels and country clubs eagerly embrace their return. The arrangements are much the same as for an evening dance. The curtains are drawn, the lights dimmed, and candles lighted.

Decorations may be as simple or elaborate as the establishment or host chooses. When the tea dance is held during a particular holiday—Valentine's Day, for example—the theme would naturally center around the color red with hearts prominently featured.

Tea sandwiches, cakes, tea, and coffee are served. Bowls of fruit punch are placed on a separate table, and a bar serves stronger drinks.

Guests go to the table and are served tea or coffee. They help themselves to the sandwiches and cakes, which they eat standing or seated at tables with friends.

The hours may vary, but it's generally accepted that tea dances take place from three to five o'clock or four to six o'clock. The time, of course, may be stretched slightly in either direction.

Part II: Taking Tea Today

Chapter Three

Hosting an Afternoon Tea at Home

There are few hours in life more agreeable than the hour dedicated to the ceremony known as afternoon tea.

HENRY JAMES
(1843–1916)

*N*o one is quite sure when afternoon tea was introduced into England, but the ceremony became widespread by the 1840s. Credit is given to Anna, seventh Duchess of Bedford, who, because of the long hours between lunch and the evening meal, suffered from afternoon "sinking spells." She remedied them with a tray of tea, bread and butter, and cake. Unable to give up her delightful new habit, she began sharing it with friends. Tea soon progressed from a simple "drink with jam and bread" into a full-blown social event among the English aristocracy.

History, however, places afternoon tea in France more than a century earlier. Madame de Sévigné (1626–1696) referred to "five o'clock tea" in a letter to a friend and mentioned her surprise that some people take milk in their tea.

The traditional time for afternoon tea is four o'clock. Today, most hotels and tearooms in North America serve from three to five o'clock with the hours often stretched slightly in either direction. Along with a choice of teas, there are three distinct courses: savories (tiny sandwiches) first to blunt the appetite, then scones, and finally, pastries. Afternoon tea has also been called "low tea" because it was taken at low tables placed beside armchairs. Please refrain from calling it "high tea" or you will find yourself in the Tea Drinkers' Hall of Shame.

An afternoon tea is a delightful and inexpensive way to entertain a small or large group. Success and enjoyment require three elements: an honest feeling of friendliness; the offering of hospitality; and the tradition of honoring the guest.

Invitations

Invitations may be extended and accepted by telephone, face-to-face, or by mailing them at least a week in advance. Depending on the geographic location, perhaps two weeks or longer in advance is not unreasonable. Invitations may be informal or engraved, handwritten in calligraphy, or by a calligraphy computer program.

Invite a close friend or two also as "pourers" and set up a schedule of when each will be "on duty" dispensing tea. No one should pour for more than fifteen or twenty minutes. It is an honor to be asked to pour tea. The pourer is considered the guardian of the teapot, which implies sterling social graces and profound trust.

Come oh come ye tea-thirsty restless ones—the kettle boils, bubbles and sings musically.

RABINDRANATH TAGORE
(1861–1941)

Time

Traditional teatime is four o'clock; however any time between two and five o'clock is appropriate for certain areas.

Guest of Honor

To get into the best society nowadays, one has either to feed people, amuse people, or shock people.

OSCAR WILDE
(1854–1900)

When you extend the invitation, let your guests know whom you are honoring.

Dialogue: "Mary, I am hosting a tea in honor of Judy Jones, and I would be pleased if you could attend."

When there is a guest of honor, it is your duty as host to stand with that person near the entrance of the room and introduce each arriving guest to the guest of honor. When the tea is over, guide your guest of honor back to the room entrance to say good-bye to your guests.

NOTE: Etiquette used to dictate that no one depart a function until the guest of honor had left the premises. The exception was when the guest of honor was also a houseguest. In today's social gatherings, you will find this rule practically nonexistent.

Dorothea Johnson

To honor

Judy Jones

Tea

Wednesday, October the fifth

Four o'clock

1401 Chain Bridge Road

McLean, Virginia

Please Respond
821-5613

Sample Invitation Sent by Mail

The protocol of the guest of honor departing first, however, is still practiced at diplomatic and official functions. At the White House, the guest of honor departs, then others are free to leave. This protocol is practiced universally at events where world leaders are in attendance.

Equipment

If it is not a large formal tea, a silver tray and tea service are not necessary. A china tea set, consisting of a teapot, a creamer for the milk, a sugar bowl, a pitcher of hot water (for those who prefer weak tea), and a plate for lemon slices arranged on a wooden or tin tray are fine. The tea tray and china tea set are placed at one end of the table. On the right, set out the necessary number of cups and saucers and teaspoons to accommodate your guests. Plates, flatware, and tea napkins are placed on the left. Platters of refreshments can include tea sandwiches in fancy shapes, various kinds of nut breads, cakes, pastries, and cookies.

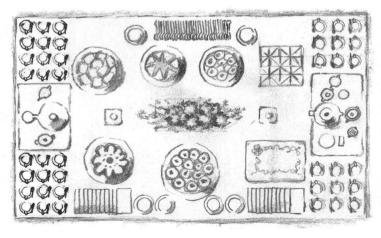

A tea table for a large group.

When the tea is small, the hostess may pour tea for a short period of time and then ask a friend to take her place. This frees her to spend more time with her guests.

Each guest tells the pourer his or her preference, i.e., strong or weak tea; tea with milk, sugar, or lemon.

The pourer serves the tea, and the guest helps himself or herself to refreshments. If it is a small tea, guests sit down. Otherwise, it is a stand-up affair.

At a large tea party, circulate around the room, talking to your guests and seeing that everyone has met and is comfortably enjoying the party.

Candles

Lighted candles add so much atmosphere to an afternoon tea, but there is a candle etiquette to be observed: Curtains are drawn when candles are lighted.

Teapots

The earliest teapots were wine jars (ewers). The Japanese and Chinese used them to hold the boiling water that was poured onto the leaves in small bowls.

Until the 1760s, most teapots made in Europe and America were of silver and intended for the rich who could afford tea.

Josiah Wedgwood perfected a method for uniformly coloring the earthenware produced by his company. His elegant plates came to the attention of England's royal family, and in 1765 Queen Charlotte commissioned him to make a tea service. The Queen gave her permission to christen his service "Queen's Ware." Before long, every aristocrat in England wanted to own Queen's Ware, just as the French patronized Sèvres and Limoges. As time passed, manufacturers began to create teapots in extravagant designs.

Flatware

Flatware is defined as flat table utensils— knives, forks, spoons, plates, platters, and so forth. Flatware is necessary at teas in the following situations.

- When serving cake that is very soft and sticky or filled with cream, forks must be laid on the tea table.
- If jam or cream is to be eaten on scones or bread, there must be knives or butter spreaders.

If two women should pour from the same pot, one of them will have a baby within the year.

TEA SUPERSTITION

- If there are dishes with jam and cream where everyone takes a portion, each dish should have its own serving spoon. One should never use one's own utensils to dip into the jam or cream dish.

- When seated at a table in a private home or in a tearoom, there should be at each place setting a knife or butter spreader on the right side of the plate and a fork on the left side. A teaspoon may be placed on the saucer holding the cup or to the right of the knife.

Teacups

The teacups you use today for your tea have handles, but this was not always the style. Chinese tea bowls influenced the first European teacups. These dainty little bowls did not have handles or saucers.

At first, the English made teacups without handles in the traditional Chinese style. Not until the mid-1750s was a handle added to the cup to prevent ladies from burning their fingers. This improvement was copied from a posset cup, which was also used for hot beverages. (A posset is a hot drink made of milk with wine, ale, or spirits.)

The saucer was once a small dish for sauce, which is how it comes by its name. Later it moved to its present position under the cup, which is now regarded as incomplete without it. In late Victorian and Edwardian days, tea drinkers poured their tea into their saucers to cool before sipping, and it was perfectly acceptable. This is what writers of the period mean by "a dish of tea." Today, this would be considered improper, and one would appear cloddish about tea drinking.

It was also proper in the late seventeenth century for a lady to signal she had sipped enough tea by laying her spoon across the top of her cup, tapping the cup lightly with the spoon, or turning the cup upside down. All of these actions are considered rather gauche today.

Two teaspoons, accidentally placed together on a saucer, points to a wedding or a pregnancy.

TEA SUPERSTITION

How to Hold Cups and Saucers

Place the saucer holding the cup in the palm of your left hand and move it forward to rest on the four fingers, which are slightly spread apart. Steady the saucer with your thumb resting on the rim. A left-handed person simply reverses the procedure.

A handled cup is held with the index finger through the handle, the thumb just above it to support the grip, and the second finger below the handle for added security. The next two fingers naturally follow the curve of the other fingers. It is an affectation to raise the little finger, even slightly.

The crooked, extended pinkie dates back to the eleventh-century Crusades and the courtly etiquette of knighthood. Since ancient Rome, a cultured person ate with three fingers, a commoner with five. Thus, the birth of the raised pinkie as a sign of elitism. This three-fingers etiquette rule is still correct when picking up food with the fingers and handling various pieces of flatware. Etiquette books, however, do not offer instructions on extending a crooked pinkie. This affectation is, no doubt, descended from a misinterpretation of the three-fingers versus five-fingers dictates of dining etiquette in the eleventh century.

Faux Pas

- Cradling the cup in one's fingers when it has a handle.
- Swirling the liquid around in the cup as if it were wine in a glass.

As dusk gave way to the first stars, the women arrived, bowing delightfully. . . . Spicy pickled fruit was passed around on cleverly shaped trays. There then appeared transparent porcelain cups, the size of half an egg, from which the ladies drank a few drops of sugarless tea poured from doll-like kettles.

PIERRE LOTI,
MADAME CHRYSANTHÈME

The Gaiwan

The *gaiwan* (Chinese covered cup) is held, when not drinking from it, very much like a teacup and saucer are held. Place the saucer holding the cup in the palm of your right hand and move it forward to rest on the four fingers, which are slightly spread apart. Steady the cup with your thumb resting on the rim. A left-handed person simply reverses the procedure.

To drink from the *gaiwan,* use the thumb and index finger of your left hand to hold the lid by its knob, and let the other three fingers follow the curve of the *gaiwan.* Tilt the lid slightly away from your lips so that it serves as a filter holding back the leaves as you drink the liquid. The cup is never removed from the saucer.

Faux Pas

- Striking the lid against the cup.

It is considered poor form in most cultures to make unnecessary noises with the accoutrements one uses while eating or drinking.

A scene in the award-winning film *The Last Emperor*, directed by Bernardo Bertolucci, emphasizes this point with great style. Several Chinese empresses have gathered in a room at the palace and are drinking tea from *gaiwans*. It is announced that the young emperor will need to

Each cup of tea represents an imaginary voyage.
CATHERINE DOUZEL

wear glasses or eventually go blind. He says decisively: "I *will* wear glasses!" Of course, it was unheard of for emperors to wear glasses. The dowager empress shows her extreme displeasure at his decision by noisily slamming the lid of her *gaiwan* onto the cup, an act of rudeness only an empress would dare to commit with such flair.

Handling the Cup and Saucer and Food Plate

When you are invited to tea in a private residence, the guests will be served tea by the host/hostess or a friend who is pouring. After taking your tea from the pourer, it is your duty to serve yourself food from the tea table.

If you are taking food on a small plate, select user-friendly, non-sticky foods that do not require a knife and fork. Find a chair and carefully sit down. Hold the saucer just above the knees and raise the cup to the lips without bending forward. Place the cup and saucer on a side table when you are ready to eat. Hold the plate just above the knees with one hand and eat with the other. When you are ready for a sip of your tea, leave the food plate carefully balanced on your knees, raise the cup and saucer from the table, and sip from the cup as described previously.

My dear, if you could give me a cup of tea to clear my muddle of a head I should better understand your affairs.

CHARLES DICKENS
(1812–1870)

If a table is not within your reach, keep the cup and saucer in your hand with the plate balanced on your knees. Remove one or two pieces of food from the plate to the side of the saucer, or eat directly from the plate. You may return for more food, and when you have finished eating, place the used plate on the tray or side table usually reserved for this purpose, never back on the tea table.

The mere clink of cups and saucers turns the mind to happy repose.

GEORGE GISSING

Faux Pas

• Lifting only the cup, leaving the saucer on the table, when you are standing.

• Lifting only the cup when you are seated and there is more than 12 inches between you and the table on which your cup and saucer are placed.

• Placing used accoutrements back on the tea table. A cup, saucer, plate, flatware, or napkin, once used, must never be placed back on the tea table. This table's primary function is for displaying the foods and the tea to be served. It should look beautiful throughout the tea. Place soiled items on the table or tray that is provided for this purpose.

Stirring a Cup of Tea

One of the most annoying sounds is a spoon hitting the inside of a cup when one is stirring.

Stirring a cup of tea is done gently and noiselessly by moving the teaspoon in a small arch back and forth in the center of the cup. Do not allow the teaspoon to touch the sides or rim of the cup. Remove the spoon and place it on the saucer behind the cup, with the handle of the spoon pointing in the same direction as the handle of the cup. Visualize the face of a clock on the saucer and properly place the handle of the cup and the handle of the spoon at four on the clock.

Faux Pas

- Leaving a spoon upright in the cup.
- Placing the spoon on the saucer in front of the cup.
- Making unnecessary noise by touching the sides of the cup with the spoon while stirring.
- Letting the spoon drop, after stirring the tea, with a clank onto the saucer.

Tea Spills in Your Saucer

In upscale establishments or someone's home, tea spills may be remedied by requesting a clean saucer. In a very casual setting, it is acceptable to fold a paper napkin and slip it under the cup to soak up the liquid. Remove the unsightly soggy napkin from the saucer and place it on another dish if one is available.

And is there honey

still for tea?

RUPERT BROOKE
(1887–1915)

When your saucer has a few droplets of tea, it is acceptable to brush the cup lightly against the saucer rim before lifting it to your lips.

You can prevent saucer spills by filling the teacup only three-quarters full.

Napkins

Wouldn't it be dreadful to live in a country where they didn't drink tea?

NOEL COWARD
(1899–1973)

The word *napkin* derives from the old French *napéron*, meaning "little tablecloth."

The first napkins were the size of today's bath towels. This size was practical because one ate the multicourse meal entirely with the fingers. The ancient Egyptians, Greeks, and Romans used them to cleanse the hands during a meal, which could last many hours. At many such meals, it was proper to provide a fresh napkin with each course to keep diners from offending each other, since it was believed they would get sick watching each other wipe their mouths on filthy napkins.

During the sixth century B.C., Roman nobility created what we now call a "doggie bag." Guests attending a banquet were expected to wrap delicacies from the table in clean napkins to take home. It was rude to depart empty-handed.

Today, in all dining situations, the napkin is properly picked up and unfolded on the lap, not above the table level. A large dinner napkin is folded in half with the fold facing the body, while a luncheon or tea napkin may be opened completely. In upscale restaurants, the wait staff are trained to place the napkin on your lap, often with too much of a flourish to suit me. Pause for a moment to make sure you and the wait staff do not reach for the napkin simultaneously.

Don't wipe your mouth with the napkin. Blot it. Lipstick is never blotted on a cloth napkin; discreetly blot the lipstick onto a tissue before you begin to eat. Don't use a napkin as a handkerchief. The napkin should remain on the lap during tea.

If you need to leave the table temporarily, place your napkin on your chair, not on the table. Push your chair back under the table if the setting is appropriate.

In upscale restaurants, the wait staff will refold the napkin and place it on the table to the left side of your plate or on the arm of your chair, a practice I thoroughly abhor, even though they are trained to handle the napkin as little as possible. Return the napkin to your lap when you are seated.

The host or hostess picks up his or her napkin to signal the close of the tea. He or she makes certain all of the guests have finished before making this move.

At the end of the tea, the napkin is not refolded but picked up by the center and placed loosely to the left of the plate.

Faux Pas

• Placing a used napkin back on the table before the meal is over.

Tea Infuser/Filter, Tea Strainer, Mote Spoon, and Caddy Spoon

• Tea infusers/filters are used to contain the leaves and permit easy removal of the used tea leaves. Some teapots are fitted with infusion baskets, also called filters. Be sure to give the leaves inside room to expand in the water when using the stainless-steel wire-mesh infusers, called "tea balls." It is advisable to employ two tea balls in making a six-cup pot. Avoid cute infusion devices made of pot metal. These often impart an unpleasant metallic taint and are, besides, inefficient.

John Harney once overheard my complaints about cleaning messy wet tea leaves from the teapot. He handed me a tea filter and said, "Try this; you'll never have to clean leaves from a teapot again." John was right, and I am very grateful to him. Tea filters work best because they

Eating is that which explains half the emotion of life.

SYDNEY SMITH
(1771–1845)

allow a lot of water to circulate without releasing the leaves into the brew. My tea-drinking friends, all former "messy tea leaf complainers," have received gifts of tea filters.

• Tea strainers are designed to be held above or to rest on top of the cup to catch leaves that escape from the teapot when the tea is poured. I still use one, even though I don't need to since the leaves are contained in my tea filter. It's the ritual of holding that little silver object over the cup, and the pouring of tea into it, that forces me to slow down and enjoy the whole process.

• A mote spoon or mote skimmer is usually made of silver with holes in the bowl. It is used to transfer tea leaves from the caddy to the teapot and also to skim off any stray leaves, or "motes," that may have escaped into the cup. The sharp point on the end is used to unblock the teapot spout if it gets clogged with tea leaves.

• Caddy spoons have short handles so they will fit in the tea caddy. They are used to convey the tea from the tea caddy to the teapot.

Proper Tea Pouring

Tea pouring involves the most stylized and personal element of the afternoon tea ceremony simply because of the intimate interaction between pourer and guest.

Tea is always served by the host/hostess or a friend, never by servants. Tea is never poured out, then passed several cups at a time, the way coffee may be, because it cools very quickly. Instead, it is always taken by the guest directly from the hands of the pourer.

Holding the teacup and saucer in his/her left hand, the pourer begins by asking each guest the following, "Do you prefer strong or weak tea?"

Strong Tea Requests

Pour the cup three-fourths full to prevent the tea spilling into the saucer. Then ask, "With milk, sugar, or lemon?" Add the requested ingredients and place a spoon on the saucer if it is not already there. (See "Milk, Sugar, and Lemon" section, which follows.)

Weak Tea Requests

Pour the cup about one-half full, leaving space for the addition of hot water. Add the hot water and then ask, "With milk, sugar, or lemon?" Add the requested ingredients and place a spoon on the saucer if it is not already there. (See "Milk, Sugar, and Lemon" section, which follows.)

Indeed, Madame, your ladyship is very sparing of your tea; I protest the last I took was no more than water bewitched.

JONATHAN SWIFT
(1667–1745)

Sugar and Lemon Requests

Add the sugar first, otherwise the citric acid of the lemon prevents it from dissolving.

When the Guest Responds, "Plain"

No addition of milk, sugar, or lemon is required. It is not necessary to place a spoon on the saucer.

The Tea Strainer

The person pouring the tea, if necessary, holds a tea strainer in one hand while lifting the teapot and pouring with the other hand.

Bubbles on tea

denote kisses.

TEA SUPERSTITION

Milk, Sugar, and Lemon

The habit of putting milk in tea reportedly started in France. Madame de Sévigné described how Madame de la Sablière launched the fashion: "Madame de la Sablière took her tea with milk, as she told me the other day, because it was to her taste."

It is a given that milk complements full-bodied India and Ceylon teas and that cream masks the taste of any tea. This settled, let's launch right into a hotly debated issue in tea etiquette:

ARE YOU AN M.I.F. (MILK IN FIRST)?
OR ARE YOU AN M.I.L. (MILK IN LAST)
TEA DRINKER?

Milk is poured after the tea. You may have heard or read that milk precedes the tea into the cup; but please, please, dear tea lovers, don't be guilty of this faux pas (another reason for banishment to the Tea Drinkers' Hall of Shame).

Don't put the milk in before the tea because then you cannot judge the strength of the tea by its color. Also, you need not hear some snobbish, chilly remark such as, "Oh, she's the milk-in-first type of person."

Where did this old milk-first tale come from? Samuel Twining has theorized that milk-first prevented early china from cracking in reaction to boiling water. That theory appears rather shaky today since boiling water is not poured directly into the cup. Boiling water is poured over tea leaves in a teapot. The leaves steep at least three minutes, producing a liquid of a temperature much reduced from the boiling stage.

GOOD REASONS TO ADD MILK
AFTER THE TEA IS POURED INTO A CUP

- The butler in the popular 1970s television program *Upstairs, Downstairs* kindly gave the following advice to the household servants who were arguing about the virtues of milk before or after the tea is poured: "Those of us downstairs put the milk in first, while those upstairs put the milk in last."

- Moyra Bremner, author of *Enquire Within Upon Modern Etiquette and Successful Behaviour*, says, "Milk, strictly speaking, goes in after the tea."

- According to the English writer Evelyn Waugh, "All nannies and many governesses . . . put the milk in first." And, by the way, Queen Elizabeth II adds the milk last.

SUGAR

Sugar cubes are preferable, not only for the ritual of using elegant sugar tongs, but for their neatness. There's nothing messier than spilled sugar granules. Allow the cube(s) to rest briefly (to dissolve) and then stir gently and noiselessly.

To put milk in your tea before sugar is to cross the path of love, perhaps never to marry.

TEA SUPERSTITION

Love and scandal

are the best

sweeteners of tea.

HENRY FIELDING
(1707–1754)
*LOVE IN SEVERAL
MASQUES*

LEMON

Lemon is agreeable with most black teas. Lovers of fragrant Earl Grey and smoky Lapsang Souchong, however, say they are best enjoyed unadulterated.

Lemon is offered thinly sliced (never in wedges!) and placed on a dish near the milk and sugar. A lemon fork (with splayed tines) or a similar serving utensil is provided. The tea pourer or the tea drinker can then put a slice directly into the poured cup of tea.

Should you desire another cup of tea, the pourer will remove the slice of lemon from your cup and pour your tea. The tea pourer or you may add a fresh lemon slice. You may also be offered a fresh cup, depending on availability.

Tip: Milk and lemon are never used together in tea. The citric acid of the lemon causes the milk to curdle.

Lemon Faux Pas

• Putting the lemon slice in the cup before pouring the tea. Tea is always poured in the cup first.

• Placing a lemon slice on the edge of the saucer in anticipation of adding it to the cup later.

• Transferring the lemon slice from the cup of tea to the saucer. You will end up with your cup resting in a puddle of tea.

• Removing the cloves from the lemon slice before placing in the teacup. The cloves are placed in the lemon slices to add flavor.

• Using the spoon to press the lemon slice after you place it in the cup. Untouched, the oil from the peel and the juice from the fruit will provide the desired essence.

Tea-Pouring Faux Pas

• Filling the cup with tea almost to the rim. This results in messy spills in the saucer, which causes dripping tea as one lifts the cup to one's lips.

Should the lid be accidentally left off the teapot, you may expect a stranger bearing ill tidings.

TEA SUPERSTITION

Chapter Four

Guest Duties at a Social Tea

*W*oody Allen has often said, "Eighty percent of success is showing up." While this may be true in certain situations, it doesn't work for the guests who show up and sit like pitchers waiting to be filled. Good guests sing for their supper, or tea as it may be. The ideal guest's virtues are evident in many subtle ways.

First, remove those gloves as soon as you step inside. One does not shake hands while wearing gloves, even if one is hankering to bring them back as a fashion statement. Please, dear tea lovers, let's look on the bright side and hope that we do not see one more woman holding a teacup with gloved hands. It has never been correct to eat or drink with gloved hands.

Gloves have been around for more than 10,000 years, and they evolved from the desire to protect the hands from cold weather and from heavy manual labor. Regardless of the climate, every major civilization eventually fabricated both work and costume gloves. Yet there is nothing to indicate they were ever worn while eating or drinking. One must remember that until the seventeenth century, food was picked up with the fingers and eaten in this fashion or speared with a knife and conveyed to the mouth. Every old etiquette book I have in my library decrees that gloves are removed for eating and drinking. Even the long gloves worn with opulent ball gowns were designed to be unbuttoned and folded back to the wrist area.

Greet your host first but don't monopolize him or her. Mingle with the other guests and introduce yourself to those you don't know. A considerate guest will also introduce those guests who do not know each other. Refer to the next sections of this chapter for social introductions and Chapter Six for business introductions.

After getting a cup of tea, help yourself to the food. You may prefer my favorite method and decide just to balance a couple of tiny sandwiches on your saucer and continue mingling. This is a great way to meet others and hone your greeting and conversational skills.

Confidence does more to make conversation than wit.

FRANÇOIS DE LA
ROCHEFOUCAULD
(1613–1680)

If there are chairs and tables and you wish to sit down, place some food on one of the small plates provided and sit down and chat with the other guests.

You may return for tea and food as often as you wish. When you have finished drinking and eating, place the cup and saucer and plate on a side table, never back on the tea table.

After an hour or so of mingling with the guests, thank the host and say good-bye to him or her and to the guest of honor.

Write a thank-you note within twenty-four hours.

Faux Pas

- Wearing gloves while shaking hands, eating, or drinking.
- Monopolizing the host or guest of honor.
- Failing to mingle with the other guests.
- Heaping too much food on the plate.
- Placing the used cup and saucer or any debris on the tea table.
- Failing to write a thank-you note.

Introducing Yourself

Introducing yourself is how you make yourself known to others. Whether in a social or business context, each time you introduce yourself, you are sharing who you are. It is your duty to introduce yourself at any function, large or small, if no one introduces you. You will never make new acquaintances or expand your horizons by holding back or talking only to people you already know. A good introduction includes your first and last name.

Social Introductions

In both formal and informal introductions, the first name spoken is that of the older or more distinguished person. The second name spoken is that of the person being introduced (or presented) to the older or more distinguished person.

Exception: Men are introduced to women with these exceptions:

According to international diplomatic protocol, women are introduced (or presented) to ambassadors, ministers in charge of legations, chiefs of state, royalty, and dignitaries of the church.

Example: "Mr. Ambassador, may I introduce (or present) Mrs. Hill. Her husband is CEO of Sky Corporation. His Excellency is the ambassador of Germany."

Formal Introductions

- Introduce a man to a woman.

Example: "Ms. Doe, may I introduce Mr. Jones. His wife is chairing tonight's event. Ms. Doe's company donated the flowers."

- Introduce a younger person to an older person.

In this case, you are presenting a child to an adult.

Example: "Mr. Smith, I would like to introduce Mary Johnson, my daughter."

Informal Introductions

To introduce two persons in a group where everyone is on a first-name basis.

Example: "Mary Smith, I want to introduce Tom Jones."

If you know only one of the two persons by his or her first name, then introduce both as Ms., Mrs., or Mr. to be consistent.

Example: "Ms. Smith, I want to introduce Mr. Jones."

Tip: Always add some information that will launch others easily into conversation.

Example: "Debbie Smith, I want to introduce Mary Hills. Mary and I were classmates in college, and she is here on business. Debbie and I are working on the museum fund-raiser."

Introducing a Number of People

Say the new person's name and then give the names of the others in the group. If you cannot remember all of their names, it is correct, acceptable, and practical to say the new person's name and suggest that the others introduce themselves.

Don't use expressions such as "shake hands with" or "make the acquaintance of."

Don't tack on "my friend" to one of the names when introducing two persons. It implies that the other person is not a friend.

If you are introducing new arrivals at a party, a round-the-room-tour is not necessary. Introduce the newcomers to the closest group of people and check from time to time to make sure they are circulating.

Family Introductions

Introducing one's spouse:

• Never refer to your own husband or wife as Mr. Smith or Mrs. Smith in social introductions. If your last name is known to everyone, all you need say is, "Tom, my husband," or "Mary, my wife."

• A man should never say, "Meet the missus" or "Meet the wife."

• If a woman has become well known by a professional name, she should mention her husband's last name when introducing him.

Example: "Mr. Jones, I want to introduce Tom Williams, my husband."

This avoids the awkwardness of the husband being called by the wife's last name.

Introducing Relatives

- Clarify their relationship to you.

Examples: "Clay Brown, I want to introduce Grant Robertson, my brother."

"Mary Smith, I want to introduce Ellen Colby, my sister-in-law."

- If one's mother has remarried, "Mary Cameron, my mother" or "Harry Cameron, my stepfather."

Chapter Five

Going Out to Tea

The spirit of the tea beverage is one of peace, comfort, and refinement.

ARTHUR GRAY

s pleasant as it is to host a tea at home, going out to tea is one of life's most delightful pastimes. A hotel lounge or tearoom may use various titles to describe its tea offerings. Menus offer *Afternoon Tea, Cream Tea, Light Tea, Full Tea, and Royal Tea.* You will also encounter an offering of *High Tea* in certain establishments in America. However, I suspect they mean *Afternoon Tea.* (Refer to high tea on page 88.)

Service Defined

Service describes the manner of presenting various dishes. Table service also takes into account the ensemble of objects that are used at the table: linens, plates, glasses, and flatware. The utensils required to serve a special part of the meal are called "services"—tea service, coffee service, dessert service, fruit service, and so forth. The French call the personnel of the restaurant who are responsible for serving meals the "service."

Cream Tea

A light repast that originated in the southwestern part of England around Devon and Cornwall, it calls only for some scones, jam, clotted cream, and choice of tea.

Light Tea

A lighter version of afternoon tea. The menu includes scones, sweets, and choice of tea.

Full Tea

A complete four-course menu includes finger sandwiches, scones, sweets, and dessert, and choice of tea. The addition of finger sandwiches (savories) as a first course gives this tea the title of "full tea."

To spill a little tea whilst making it is a lucky omen.

TEA SUPERSTITION

Royal Tea

Choice of tea and a four-course menu of finger sandwiches, scones, sweets, dessert, and a glass of champagne or sherry. The addition of a glass of champagne or sherry gives this tea the distinction of being called "royal tea."

High Tea

The term "high tea" is often misused by those who like to gild afternoon tea to make it seem exclusive and refined. Consequently, both consumers and dispensers of tea often mistakenly tack the word "high" onto what should be simply called tea or afternoon tea.

Although often confused with afternoon tea, high tea is not a dainty affair, neither is it synonymous with highbrow. The distinction is important if you wish to convey a certain degree of sophistication. High tea is NOT finger sandwiches, scones, and sweets. That, of course, is tea or afternoon tea.

High tea is a hearty, simple, sit-down meal that originated during the Industrial Revolution of the nineteenth century. High tea was the main meal of the day for workers who returned home very hungry after a long, hard day in the fields, shops, factories, and mines.

Everything is placed on the table, family style, and dishes are passed from person to person. The menu offers hot or cold hearty and traditional foods such as meat pies, Welsh rarebit, sausage, cold meats, breads, cheese, jam, butter, relishes, desserts, fruits, and tea. High tea was also called "meat tea," because meat was usually served.

One may offer "high tea" in the form of a buffet supper, and alcohol may also be served.

Tea in a Hotel Lounge

You will often be seated on a sofa or an overstuffed chair. A low table (coffee table) in front of the sofa will hold the tea foods, cups and saucers, and pot(s) of tea. You may eat in the same manner as you would at a regular table. Should you sit back in your seat and there is an uncomfortable distance between you and your teacup, be sure to lift both the cup and saucer from the table as previously described.

Chapter Six

Business Etiquette & Tea

Bring me a cup of tea and the Times.

QUEEN VICTORIA'S
FIRST COMMAND
UPON HER ACCESSION
TO THE THRONE

*A*fternoon tea is fashionable and trendy, not just as a social function but as a professional one as well. In their search for a quiet place to wheel and deal, executives are leading a briefcase invasion of the genteel sanctuaries once the preserves of white-gloved ladies. Men and women are learning to say to clients and business associates, "Let's discuss this over tea," instead of setting a luncheon date.

There is, after all, a relaxing, albeit powerful, quality to closing deals over a cup of tea, watercress sandwiches, and scones slathered with strawberry jam and clotted cream. While teatime does involve food and drink, it is the opposite of the business lunch or dinner, both of which can be expensive, complicated, caloric, and intoxicating.

Extending the Invitation

You may invite over the telephone or face-to-face a week in advance or as close as one day beforehand. When you extend the invitation, be precise about the time, place, and the purpose of your invitation. Since each person has his or her own agenda, the guest will want to come prepared. Let your guest know if you will meet in the lobby or at your reserved table.

The Host or Hostess

It is the duty of a host or hostess to handle the smallest detail, from the reservation to the tip, for both the tea and any items left with the coat-room attendant. Additional duties include leading the conversation. Maintain complete control when you are hosting. There should never be any doubt by the staff at your selected site that you are the host.

Pre-Tea Strategy

• Know the hotel lounge or tearoom you are using. Before the day of your business tea, visit the site if it is new to you. Introduce yourself to the maître d' (or captain).

A host is like a general:
It takes a mishap to
reveal his genius.
HORACE

- Pick your table. Select the table at which you wish to be seated and which gives you maximum privacy when you expect to discuss business. Decide where your guest(s) will sit and where you plan to sit.

- Alert the maître d' or captain to your preferred seating arrangement by saying, "My guest will sit there and I will sit here; please pull out the chair for my guest first."

- Always avoid: a table facing a mirror, a table next to the kitchen, and a table near the restrooms.

The Day of Your Tea

The morning of your tea meeting, reconfirm the time and place with your guest or his or her secretary. Since reservations get mixed up, reconfirm with the hotel lounge or tearoom you are using as well.

Change of Plans

If you or your guest must reschedule your meeting, call the hotel lounge or tearoom and cancel your reservation. Failure to do so makes you appear unprofessional and inconsiderate. Honor a tea reservation just as you would a business appointment.

Arrive Early

Plan to arrive at least fifteen minutes early to check the table and arrange payment of the check with the maître d' or captain. You may sign the check beforehand or ask the captain to hold it for you at his or her station. Excuse yourself from the table as teatime is drawing to a close and take care of the check. Should your guest express concern about the check not being presented, you can simply smile and say, "It has been taken care of." This is a polished method that anyone can use effectively any place and for any function. An added bonus is the fact that it efficiently solves the problem of a male guest insisting on picking up the check when the host is female. By depersonalizing the event, it is no longer a gender issue. After all, business protocol dictates that the person who does the inviting pays, regardless of gender.

Lobby Meeting

Greet your guest with a handshake and usher him or her ahead of you as you are led to your table. Always offer your guest the preferred seat. It should be the one first pulled from the table, facing out into the room.

It isn't the menu that

matters, it's the men

you sit next to.

MAE WEST

When there are only two of you at tea, don't sit across from each other at a square or round table; it is too confrontational. Seat your guest to your right.

When hosting two guests, and the table accommodates four, don't place one guest on each side of you. To do so means you will be moving your head back and forth as if you were at a tennis match. Place the senior person on your right and the junior person across from you, leaving the place on your left empty.

If there are others in your party, indicate where you would like them to sit, and see that everyone is seated before you sit down.

Faux Pas

- Saying to your guest, "Just sit anyplace."
- Involving your guest in paying the check.

Table Meeting

Inform the maître d' or captain that your guest, Mr. Doe, will be joining you at your table. Upon arrival, he will be shown to your table. This is an easy way to recognize a guest you've never seen before.

Regardless of gender, the host stands when the guest(s) approach(es) the table and remains standing until everyone at the table is seated.

The Social Side of a Business Tea

The business tea is gaining popularity, and professionals at all levels need to be aware of the social nuances involved. There is always a slight social overtone to tea even though business is being discussed. A professional woman should never assume that a male colleague will pull out her chair; but if he does, she accepts graciously.

Taking Your Seat at a Table

Both women and men use the same method to take a seat.

Move to the right of your chair and enter from your left side. Your left hip touches the chair first. (*Exception:* When the chair is pulled out and space doesn't permit entering from the right side. Be alert to the situation.) Exit the chair from the same side you entered. Always push the chair back in after you rise.

A Man Helping a Woman to Be Seated

Stand directly behind the chair, with both hands grasping the chair back. Gently pull out the chair. When the woman is half-seated, carefully push the chair in under her. Don't push it in too far. Once settled in, she can adjust it. Release the back of the chair and seat yourself to her left. (If the woman on your left has no one to seat her, you will also seat her.)

Carry yourself as if you paid a million bucks, and you got a bargain.

HESTER PROVENSEN

A Woman Being Helped with Her Chair

Move to the right of your chair and enter from your left side. Once the chair has been pulled out and you are half-seated, grasp the sides of the seat and lean your body forward while the chair is being pushed in.

If you arrive at the table before anyone else, just seat yourself. A nearby wait staff will likely offer to pull out your chair.

When the Tea Is Over

Man: Push back your chair, rise, and reposition it at the table. Then stand behind the chair of the woman on your right, pull back her chair, and reposition it after she rises and moves away from the immediate area. You should also help the woman on your left, if necessary.

The Guest

Be an appreciative guest and participate in the conversation in a professional manner. Concentrate on your host's agenda.

Thank your host through a handwritten thank-you note on a correspondence card. Mail it within twenty-four hours. This action will garner you the title "World-Class Executive."

Tip: Every executive should have a supply of correspondence cards. Visit your local stationery store and view their selection. The cards measure $4^{1}/_{4}"$ x $6^{3}/_{8}"$.

Sample thank-you note

Making a Professional Entrance

Almost everyone watches the entrance to a room. Use it to your advantage when you go to tea. Avoid rushing into the room even if you are a little late. Maintain good posture at all times because it instantly creates an impression of confidence.

To make a strong entrance, walk into the room and pause briefly to spot key persons and to allow others to see you. Don't stand in the doorway, but walk a few feet into the room so you don't block the entrance.

Handshaking—The Ultimate Greeting

We notice persons nonverbally by their touch, and the way we touch someone socially and in business is most often with our handshake. Shaking hands easily and often creates a favorable impression and influences others to shake hands. The handshake is important because it is the accepted business greeting in almost all countries.

In America's business arena, it doesn't matter who offers a hand first. The person who extends a hand first has a distinct advantage. He or she is being direct, taking the initiative, and establishing control. These are all cutting-edge pluses in the business arena.

Handshakes are the physical greetings that go with your words.

UNKNOWN

In European countries the woman offers her hand first. When a North American business-woman fails to extend her hand to a European male executive, she loses credibility.

Always Shake Hands

- When introduced to a person and when you say good-bye;
- When someone comes into your office to see you;
- When you meet someone outside your office or home;
- When you enter a room, are greeted by those you know, and are introduced to those you don't know;
- When you leave a gathering attended by business associates;
- When you are congratulating someone who has won an award or given a speech;
- With those nearest you, your host and hostess, and with whomever you meet;
- When you are consoling someone.

Business Introductions

In business introductions, who is introduced to whom is determined by precedence. The person who holds the highest position in an organization takes precedence over others who work there. Gender does not affect the order of introductions. Women and men should be treated according to business protocol, not chivalry.

Introduce Yourself

Introduce yourself by extending your hand; smile and say, "I'm John Doe." Always use both names and never give yourself an honorific such as "I'm Mr. Doe."

Formulas for Introductions

• Persons of lesser authority are introduced to persons of greater authority, regardless of gender.

Example: "Mr./Ms. Greater Authority, I would like to introduce Mr./Ms. Lesser Authority."

Protocol: The name of the person of greater authority is always spoken first. The name of the person of lesser authority is always spoken last.

Tip: Don't reverse the order.

Explanation: If you introduce Greater to Lesser, you reverse the order.

Incorrect: Mr./Ms. Greater Authority, I would like to introduce [you to] Mr./Ms. Lesser Authority.

• A junior executive is introduced to a senior executive.

Example: "Mr. Senior Executive, I would like to introduce Ms. Junior Executive, from the accounting department. Mr. Senior Executive is our director of public relations."

Protocol: The name of the senior executive is always spoken first. The name of the junior executive is always spoken last.

Tip: Don't reverse the order.

• A fellow executive is introduced **to** a client.

Example: "Mary Hopkins, I would like to introduce Jim Smith, my department manager. Jim, Mary is our good customer from Chicago, and she is doing a brisk business with our new interactive software."

Protocol: Clients are considered more important than anyone in your organization, even if your department manager is a vice president and your client is a junior executive.

Tip: Don't reverse the order.

• A nonofficial person is introduced **to** an official person.

Example: "Senator Warner, may I introduce Ms. Doe, president of Doe Exports. Ms. Doe's firm is one of our state's leading exporters."

Protocol: The name of the official is always spoken first. The name of the nonofficial is always spoken last.

Tip: Don't reverse the order.

Introduction Savvy

• While making the introduction, refrain from making unnecessary gestures such as touching the people you are introducing or gesturing toward them when you say their names. The less you rely on gestures, the more confident and authoritative you will appear.

• Look at each person as you say his or her name. This focuses attention on the individual and makes him or her feel important while you look in control.

Handling Purses, Briefcases, Eyeglasses, and Eyeglass Cases

Simply stated, don't place any of these items on the table at which you are taking tea. Only the tea accoutrements belong on the table.

PURSES AND BRIEFCASES

Small purses go on your lap under the napkin. Large purses and briefcases are placed by your chair out of the path of the other guests and the wait staff. In a public tearoom or hotel lounge, the safest place for a large purse or briefcase is between your feet.

If you're going to play the game, you better know the rules.
BARBARA JORDAN

EYEGLASSES AND EYEGLASS CASES

An eyeglass case belongs in your purse, pocket, or briefcase. Should you feel the need to remove your glasses, place them in your jacket pocket or on your lap—never on the table.

The Do's of Tea Etiquette— Business and Social

The Do's

• Do rise, regardless of gender, to greet and shake hands with your guests.

• Do try a little of each course served at tea.

• Do avoid talking with your mouth full. Take small bites, and you will find it is easier to answer questions or join in table talk.

• Do wait until you have swallowed the food in your mouth before you take a sip of tea.

• Do place your napkin on your chair when you briefly leave the table.

• Do place your knife and fork in the 10:20 "I am finished" position when you have finished eating. Visualize a clock face on your plate. Place the tips of the utensils at the number ten and the handles at the four.

• Do carry food to your mouth with an inward, not an outward, curve of the fork.

• Do look into, not over, the cup of tea when drinking.

• Do spread the scone with jam first and then cream.

Experience is the worst teacher; it gives the test before the lesson.

VERNON LAW

The Don'ts of Tea Etiquette— Business and Social

• Don't place items on the table. This protocol extends to keys, hats, gloves, eyeglasses, eyeglass cases, anything that is not part of the meal.

• Don't overload the fork when eating the foods served at tea.

• Don't chew with your mouth open.

• Don't smack your lips.

• Don't touch your face or head during teatime.

• Don't tip up the cup too much when drinking tea, but keep it at a slight angle.

• Don't extend a pinkie when holding a cup.

• Don't reach across the table or across another person to get something. If it is out of reach, ask the closest person to pass it to you.

• Don't try to remove food from your teeth in the presence of others. If something gets caught in your teeth, excuse yourself and take care of the problem in the privacy of the restroom.

• Don't push your plate away from you at the end of the tea.

• Don't gesture with a knife, fork, or spoon in your hand. If you are not using the utensil, put it down.

• Don't talk about your personal food likes and dislikes during tea.

• Don't place your napkin on the table until you are ready to leave.

• Don't involve your guest(s) in paying the bill.

Part III: Tea & Trimmings

Chapter Seven

Finessing the Food at Tea

. . . and though I distinctly asked for bread and butter, you have given me cake!

OSCAR WILDE
(1854–1900)
THE IMPORTANCE
OF BEING EARNEST

*T*ea food is served either in separate courses or on a tiered stand. My preference is the tiered stand, which allows me to take small helpings if I am going out to dinner later. Correctly positioned, the foods are:

- First tier (bottom): tea sandwiches, which are referred to as savories.
- Second tier (middle): scones, pound cake.
- Third tier (top): pastries, tarts, or any dessert-type sweet.

Begin at the bottom tier and work your way up.

Tea Sandwiches (Savories)

The notorious eighteenth-century gambler John Montagu, fourth Earl of Sandwich, is credited with inventing the sandwich.

In 1762, when Montagu was forty-four years old, his passion for gambling kept him at the gaming tables for twenty-four straight hours.

To keep gambling, he ordered sliced meats and cheeses served to him between pieces of bread. This method enabled him to eat with one hand and gamble with the other.

Tea sandwiches are savory, tasty tidbits eaten first to blunt the appetite. They may be open-faced or closed sandwiches consisting of cucumbers, chicken salad, salmon, hummus, tomatoes, and so forth.

Scones

Scones are simple biscuits, often made with currants. I will describe several methods of eating scones, all of them correct, but some hands-on preparation on the part of diners is required.

• Using the knife, slice through the scone horizontally, resting it flat on your plate. Spoon small dollops (just enough for a single scone) of jam and cream onto your plate. Never spoon directly onto the scone. Take only the amount of topping needed to eat that one scone and spread one bite at a time, not over the whole scone. Use your knife to dab the edge of the scone with jam, then cream; eat that portion and return the rest to your plate. Sip a little tea, make brilliant conversation, spread new jam and cream, and take another bite, and so on. Between bites, rest the knife on the upper right side of your plate, with the cutting side of the blade facing in. When you have finished, place the knife in the "I am finished" position. (Visualize the face of a clock on your plate. Place the knife in the 10:20 position. The tip of the knife is at ten and the handle is at four. The cutting side of the knife blade always faces in.)

• Slice through the scone, on your plate; lift off the top piece. Using the knife, spread only the bottom half first with jam and then cream. Place the knife on the upper right side of your plate. You may pick this half of the scone up with your hand, but be ready to use your napkin for those tell-tale signs of cream and jam around the mouth area. This is not a pretty sight! When you have finished, place the knife in the "I am finished" position described above.

• Slice through the scone on your plate, lift off the top piece, and break off a bite-size piece with your fingers. Use your knife to spread on jam, then cream, and convey to the mouth with your fingers. Between bites, place the knife on the upper right side of your plate, with the cutting side of the blade facing in. Repeat the procedure with bite-size pieces. When you have finished, place the knife in the "I am finished" position.

• If you don't wish to eat the scone with your fingers, try one of the following styles:

American style: Slice through the scone and lift off the top piece and spread only this half, first with jam and then cream. Secure the scone with the fork in your left hand. With your right hand, use the knife to cut a bite-size piece. Place the knife on the upper right side of your plate and switch the fork to the right hand. Lift the bite with your fork and convey it to your mouth.

When you have finished, place the knife and fork in the "I am finished" position. (Visualize the face of a clock on your plate. Place both the knife and fork in the 10:20 position with the tines of the fork up. The tip of the knife and fork are at the ten and the handles are at the four. The knife is on the outside, and the cutting side of the blade faces the fork, which is on the inside.)

Continental style: Slice through the scone and lift off the top piece. Spread only this half, first with jam and then cream. Secure the scone with the fork in your left hand. With the knife in your right hand, cut a bite-size piece and convey it to your mouth with the fork in the left hand, tines down. The knife remains in the right hand. Cut only one bite at a time. Should you wish to rest and sip tea, the fork and knife are crossed on the plate with the fork over the knife with the tines pointed down. Picture an inverted "V."

When you have finished, place the knife and fork in the 10:20 position with the tines of the fork down. The tip of the knife and fork are at the number ten, and the handles are at the four. The knife is on the outside, and the cutting side of the blade faces the fork, which is on the inside.

Fact: In the United Kingdom, scones are not always served at tea; neither are they always served with cream. They are often offered with butter and jam or honey. Spread the butter first and the jam or honey last. In some regions scones with currants are served only with butter.

Faux Pas

• Putting the scone halves back together, like a sandwich, after spreading on the jam and cream.

Cream

The cream may be called clotted cream, Devon cream, Devonshire cream, or whipped cream. The first three names describe the same super-rich cream imported from Devon, England. If you are served whipped cream, it should be freshly whipped. Use just a dollop on top of the jam as you prepare the scone before eating.

Pastries and Tarts

You may use your fingers unless the pastries or tarts are overfilled with cream or otherwise unwieldy. For the latter, secure the pastry or tart with the fork and use the knife to cut one bite-size piece at a time. Convey each bite to your mouth with the fork. You may eat the pastries and tarts in either the American or Continental style.

Iced Tea

Iced tea was invented quite by accident in the summer of 1904 at the St. Louis World's Fair by an Englishman, Richard Blechynden. Representing teas grown in India, he was there hoping to popularize hot tea.

The hot, humid weather created a steady stream of visitors to the cold refreshment stands offering lemonade, but day after day no one wanted Mr. Blechynden's hot tea. In desperation, he finally filled glasses with ice and poured his hot tea into them. This cool, refreshing beverage was an instant hit with the fair-goers, who carried a taste for it home with them throughout the United States.

Call it *iced* tea, not *ice* tea. Tea with ice in it is an "iced" beverage.

A GLASS OF ICED TEA

Iced tea should be served in a tall glass that is placed on a saucer or a small plate such as a bread and butter plate. The long iced teaspoon is placed on the outer right of the flatware. You may even place it at a slight angle for additional interest. Should you use the spoon to stir your tea after adding sugar, place it on the saucer.

Handling the iced teaspoon when there is no saucer to hold it after stirring is easier to demonstrate than to describe. Keep the long iced teaspoon in your glass, after you stir, with the handle held toward the far side by the index finger and with the remaining three fingers and thumb of the hand hold the glass while you drink. This is less complicated than it sounds—you quickly absorb this method and before long your gestures are fluid and you will see that it works beautifully. It is the only possible method when there is no small plate. Practice and those around you will marvel, "Oh, it must be correct because it is handled with such elegance and grace."

This is quite practical since a wet spoon may damage a bare table top or stain fine linens. The etiquette of flatware is that, once used, it should never touch the table again.

In a restaurant you may certainly ask for a saucer to place under your glass of iced tea.

Silk Tea Bags

An American, Thomas Sullivan, is credited with creating the tea bag by accident around 1908. To increase product interest, he started sending his retail customers small samples of tea in small hand-sewn silk bags. To his surprise, his customers requested more "bagged" tea, and soon Mr. Sullivan substituted gauze for the silk bag. Today, filter paper has replaced the gauze.

Finessing a Tea Bag

In a restaurant:

• When the tea bag is served with a small teapot of water and a cup and saucer: Remove the tea bag from its paper wrapper, place it in the teapot of water, and allow it to steep until it reaches the strength you prefer. After three to five minutes, pour a small amount into your cup to test the strength. Don't pick up the tea bag by the tab on the string and jiggle it up and down to hasten the process. This looks tacky and gives the appearance of impatience. Do not remove the tea bag from the teapot. Fold the tea bag wrapper and place it next to the saucer holding the teapot. If you simply can't bear to look at it, fold it and slide it under the saucer holding the teapot.

Tip: When ordering tea, you may ask your server if the hot water will be served in a teapot. If the answer is yes, request that the tea bag be placed in the teapot first and the hot water added. You will get a better infusion. (Increase your gratuity for this extra service.)

• When a cup of hot water is served with a tea bag placed on the saucer: Remove the tea bag from its paper wrapper and place in the cup of hot water. Allow the tea to steep until it reaches the strength you prefer. Request a saucer to hold the used tea bag. Don't place it on your saucer where it will drain and you will end up with a dripping cup. Never attempt to drain a tea bag by winding the string around a spoon.

• Sugar in wrappers and milk in disposable plastic containers: Request a saucer to hold the disposable wrappers and milk containers if one is not provided.

Faux Pas

• Picking up the tea bag by the tab on the string and jiggling it up and down to hasten the steeping process. It doesn't!

• Removing the tea bag from the teapot and placing it on the saucer. This looks messy and you will have a puddle of tea in your saucer which will produce a dripping teacup when you lift it.

• Draining a tea bag by winding the string around a spoon. This act places one firmly in the Tea Drinkers' Hall of Shame.

Chapter Eight
Brewing Tea

Polly put the kettle on,

we'll all have tea.

CHARLES DICKENS
(1745–1814)

*A*few simple steps make the difference between an excellent cup of tea and an ordinary one. The essential ingredients are an earthenware, porcelain, or glass teapot, good tea leaves, fresh water, and timing. If water has a high mineral content, a slightly longer steeping time may be needed since tea does not infuse as easily in hard water. On the other hand, it is more flavorful.

The Proper Way to Brew a Pot of Black Tea

• Run cold water from the faucet for at least one minute. Then fill the tea kettle with sufficient water to warm the teapot and make the tea.

• With connoisseur-quality teas, always use bottled water in your tea kettle.

• When the water is near boiling, pour some into the teapot and swirl it around to warm the teapot.

• At this stage, decide if you will place the leaves directly into the teapot or if you will use a tea infuser or filter. Many teapots come equipped with removable infusion baskets.

• Measure a rounded teaspoon of tea for each cup of water the teapot holds. Add an extra teaspoon if a strong tea is preferred.

• When the water comes to a full rolling boil, take the teapot to the kettle and pour the water onto the tea leaves. Cover the teapot and allow the tea to steep for the right length of time. A timer is recommended.

• How long to steep? Steeping time depends on the size of the leaf. Large leaves require longer steeping. Small leaves steep more quickly. Any black tea should steep at least three

The hot water is to remain upon it (the tea) no longer than whiles you can say the Miserere [Psalm 51] very leisurely.

SIR KENELM DIGBY
(1603–1665)

minutes; very few require more than six minutes. Formosa oolong calls for seven minutes, and most green teas about one minute.

Tip: If you put the leaves directly into the teapot, stir the liquid and strain or decant the steeped tea into another heated teapot. A bitter-tasting "stewy" tea will result from liquor left on the leaves for a long period of time.

How to Brew Tea in a Gaiwan *(Chinese Covered Cup)*

We can thank Norwood Pratt for educating thousands of North Americans about what he describes as "this ingenious invention," the *gaiwan.*

Gaiwan is Mandarin for "covered bowl." In use since about 1350, it consists of a saucer, bowl, and lid, which are used together.

Norwood instructs his students to place enough tea for a single cup in the bottom of the cup. With black tea or oolong, the leaves must be rinsed as if they had dust on them.

Pour in enough boiling water to fill the cup less than half full, and immediately drain off.

To stir the tea in the pot counter-clockwise will stir up trouble.

TEA SUPERSTITION

Hold the cup and saucer together and tilt the lid to hold back the leaf as you pour. Bring the *gaiwan* to your nose and uncover it to breathe in the freshly released aroma of the leaf. Pour on boiling water again, cover the cup with the lid, and steep for about three minutes.

If brewing green or white teas, omit rinsing the leaves and steep the tea without replacing the lid. Pour the water on one side of the *gaiwan,* not directly onto the tea. This method produces a swirl in the cup. Leave the cup uncovered, steep for a minute or two, and then drink.

(Refer to page 64 for instructions about drinking from a *gaiwan.*)

Tea Counts as a Vegetable

John Weisburger, a prominent cancer researcher and director emeritus of the American Health Foundation, drinks about five cups of tea a day. He says they deliver as much antioxidant punch as two fruits or vegetables. Tea's chemicals, in hot or iced tea, may help counteract carcinogens in food, notably in grilled, fried, or broiled meat.

To make tea stronger than usual, indicates a new friendship.
TEA SUPERSTITION

Tea's Antioxidant Powers

Antioxidants, called "flavonoids," combat "free radicals" linked to cancer, early aging, and other ills. Green teas are thought to supply more antioxidants than black teas.

John Folts, a University of Wisconsin cardiologist who directs the medical school's Coronary Thrombosis Research Laboratory, defines flavonoids as vitamin-like substances found in tea, red wine, and dark beer, as well as in such wholesome foods as apples, kale, and broccoli. Like vitamins C and E and beta-carotene, they are antioxidants—substances that inhibit a chemical reaction called oxidation that, among other things, can make the body's cells less resistant to cancer-causing agents. In fact, some of the flavonoids in tea are stronger antioxidants than these vitamins.

Antioxidants are good for the heart and blood vessels in two ways, Folts said:

> *They prevent the oxidation of LDL cholesterol, which is good because oxidized cholesterol is more damaging to blood vessel walls and more likely to generate plaque. Second, they reduce the clotting tendency of blood.*

Tea, although an oriental, is a gentleman at least; cocoa is a cad and coward, cocoa is a vulgar beast.

G. K. CHESTERTON
(1874–1936)

Tea Is a Healthy Aid

Tea drinkers have a lower risk of stroke reports a 1996 study in the American Medical Association *Archives of Internal Medicine*. A 25-year-long Dutch study of 552 men suggests that tea drinking protects against stroke:

> *Men who drink more than 4.7 cups of tea per day had a 60% reduced risk of stroke compared with men who drink less than 2.6 cups per day.*

Again, the compounds called flavonoids, abundant in tea and in certain fruits and vegetables, were given credit for this effect. Steven Levine, a professor of neurology and director of Stroke Service at the Henry Ford Hospital in Detroit, said the results need corroboration by further studies. The same research team had already reported in 1993 that flavonoids reduced coronary heart disease risk in elderly Dutch men.

Chapter Nine

Tea Types

Tea has a myriad of shapes. If I may speak vulgarly and rashly, tea may shrink and crinkle like a Mongol's boots. Or its leaves may look like the dewlap of a wild ox, some sharp, some curling as the eaves of a house. . . . Still others will twist and turn like the rivulets carved out by a violent rain on newly tilled fields. Those are the very finest of teas.

LU YU
EIGHTH-CENTURY
CHINESE POET

*T*here are three primary types of tea: black (fermented), oolong (partially fermented), and green (unfermented).

The taste of tea is chiefly the result of the type of leaf used and the degree or absence of fermentation.

Black Teas

Plucked green leaf is strewn in troughs and allowed to wither for periods up to twenty-four hours. Withering allows much of the moisture content to evaporate and renders the leaf limp and pliable enough to withstand manipulation. Withered leaf is then rolled by special machines that rupture the leaf cells and allow its juices and enzymes to be exposed to the air. This exposure of the juice to the air produces oxidation, which has always been misnamed "fermentation" by tea makers. As oxidation proceeds, the plant juices undergo a chemical change while at the same time the leaf gradually turns from green to brown. The tea maker, judging by the aroma of the leaf, determines when the "fermentation" is complete and the leaf is ready for "firing." Firing machines apply heat to arrest any further chemical change and dry the leaf. This dry leaf is now sorted into different "grades," or sizes of leaf, and this completes the manufacturing process.

Unlike others, black teas may be enjoyed with milk, sugar, or lemon added if desired.

ASSAM

A robust tea from Northeast India.

DARJEELING

A wonderfully delicate Indian tea from the foothills of the Himalayas, grown at altitudes up to 6,500 feet. The best are usually sold under the name of the producing estate and may be designated "First Flush" or "Second Flush" to indicate the spring or summer crop, which have distinctly different characters.

NILGIRI

Another classic high-grown tea from Nilgiri, or "Blue Mountains," of southern India.

CEYLON

Sri Lanka's great black teas, which are often sold by district or estate names or sometimes simply designated Orange Pekoe.

ORANGE PEKOE

This indicates a particular grade, i.e., size, of leaf. It is not a "type" of tea, for any black tea is available in Orange Pekoe grade. Sir Thomas Lipton popularized the term in marketing his Ceylon tea, with which it continues to be associated.

EARL GREY

May be made from almost any black tea by the addition of oil of bergamot, a Mediterranean citrus fruit used only for its scent.

ENGLISH BREAKFAST

A generic blend of teas, usually Ceylon, China, or India, which may vary wildly in quality.

IRISH BREAKFAST

Another generic blend often using Assam and African teas for a heartier, more robust cup than English Breakfast.

KEEMUN

One of the best and most famous of China's black teas, with a distinctive, subtly sweet aroma and flavor.

YUNNAN

Another great China black tea characterized by khaki-colored tips in the dry leaf and a peppery quality to the flavor.

LAPSANG SOUCHONG

A hearty, smoky, distinctively flavored South China tea.

Oolong Teas

Oolong is the semifermented type of tea, which makes it roughly halfway between the fully fermented black teas and the completely unfermented green teas. After withering, the leaf is rolled (often by hand) and fired, then allowed to cool and rolled some more and subjected to further firing at progressively cooler temperatures. This process may be repeated up to a dozen times for the finest oolongs. The resulting dry leaf resembles loosely twisted balls that vary in darkness of color depending on the degree of fermentation. Highly fermented and fired oolongs like Formosa Oolong or Ti Kuan Yin yield reddish liquors not dissimilar to black tea. More lightly fermented oolongs produce golden or paler-colored liquors. Oolongs are the most fragrant of teas and are always drunk unadulterated.

FORMOSA OOLONG

Unique to Taiwan and sometimes still called "champagne oolong" or "the champagne of teas," this prized tea is identifiable by its amber liquor and aroma of peaches.

TI KUAN YIN

This most prized mainland China oolong comes chiefly from Fujian province directly across the straits from Taiwan. The name is translated "Iron Goddess of Mercy."

SHUIXIAN, DA HONG PAO, FENGHUANG DANCONG

Other classic oolongs from mainland China, each excellent and recognizably different from all others.

DARJEELING OOLONG

A few innovative tea makers in India's Darjeeling district have begun producing less than-fully-fermented versions of their famous black tea. It is interesting and flavorful but impossible to confuse with any classic oolong.

Green Teas

Once the freshly plucked leaf has withered enough to bend without breaking, it is immediately subjected to heat, usually by being thrown into hot woks where it is stirred very fast to prevent scorching and sticking. As it dries, the leaf is rolled until eventually it rustles like paper. Different rolling techniques result in the many different twists possible in the finished leaf. As recently as the 1960s, all China green tea (perhaps three-quarters of its total production) was made entirely by hand. While machines have taken over much green leaf manufacture, China's best is still hand-made for the most part. Because the leaf is not allowed to oxidize, or "ferment," it retains its green color and all its chemical constituents in their unaltered, or unoxidized, state. Thus green tea is the nectar of the plant in its most natural form, with significantly more vitamin C, chlorophyll, and mineral content than other types of tea. For this reason it also goes stale more quickly than other teas and should be bought in small quantities and consumed fairly quickly.

The liquors are typically pale greenish or yellow and have a distinctive vegetative aroma and flavor. Green tea is an acquired taste for most Americans, but it is by far the subtlest type of all teas. It is taken without the addition of any milk, lemon, or sugar. Green tea should be prepared with water about thirty degrees below the boiling point and steeped for a minute, more or less, before the liquor is poured off the leaf, which may be used again and again for repeated infusions. The Chinese traditionally make one cup at a time using the combination brewing vessel and drinking cup called a *gaiwan*, which permits ideal control of steeping time and is replenished with hot water as needed.

Dragon Well

(Lung Ching or "Longjing" in Chinese) This most famous China green tea is prized for its "four uniques:" jade color, vegetative aroma,

chestnutty flavor, and flat-shaped leaf. The best can be very expensive and well worth it.

PI LO CHUN, HUANGSHAN MAO FENG, AND LIUAN GUAPIAN

Three more of China's most famous green teas, each delicately different.

GUNPOWDER

Known to the Chinese as "Pearl Tea" from its round, pellet-like shape, Gunpowder is probably the most widely available China green tea, which is a shame because it is also the most astringent and least subtle. It became popular before the days of modern transportation, because green tea made in this form has the longest shelf life.

HYSON

Hyson or Young Hyson (Old English trade name for Chunmee) is the commonest type of China green. "Special Chunmee" is often worth seeking out.

SENCHA

Japan's national drink, this form of green tea is noticeably grassy-tasting and light-bodied. The best quality is expensive and rarely found in the United States, but average-quality Sencha is a perfectly suitable accompaniment to sushi and other Japanese fare.

White Teas

Though sometimes imitated in Ceylon or India, white tea almost always comes from China, where it is mostly produced in Fujian province. The leaf is treated by steaming, and then it is sun-dried. White teas are best made with water well below boiling, but cannot be rendered undrinkable in any case. They are virtually without caffeine and are taken without additives.

BAI MUDAN OR WHITE PEONY

Many leaves laced together to form a "peony flower," which swells and "blossoms" once infused in the *gaiwan*. Prized more for appearance than taste, this tea should never be made in a teapot, where its unique appearance is lost.

SILVERY TIP PEKOE

Also sold as China White and Fujian White, this tea is known in Chinese as *Yinzhen* ("Silver Needles") because it is made from unopened and unusually long leaf buds. Very fresh and faintly sweet-tasting, the liquor is barely stained with a pale gold color. The imitations now made in Sri Lanka and Darjeeling are notably inferior.

PAI MU TAN

(White Peony) Clusters of tiny white flowers and gray-green leaves produce a yellow-orange brew with a sweet taste.

Scented and Flavored Teas

These are not identical. Scented teas may be green or black or even oolong. Jasmine, for instance, is green tea that has been scented with the aroma of jasmine blossoms. These are generally removed, though sometimes left mingled with the tea leaves for appearance. Jasmine tea ranges from vile to wonderful, depending on the quality of tea used as a base. Earl Grey is a scented black tea with similar variations in quality. Its distinctive scent results from spraying the leaf with essence of bergamot, a Mediterranean citrus. Rose and Lichee are the other best-known scented teas. Flavored teas, on the other hand, are almost invariably black teas that have been sprayed with natural or artificial flavors like raspberry, kiwi, watermelon, or what have you. Better-quality teas are almost never used for this purpose, and purists tend to avoid flavored teas. Flavored teas are easy to enjoy for soda-loving Americans who ordinarily don't drink tea, and it must be admitted some of them can be very pleasant as iced or dessert teas.

Herbal Tisanes

Sassafras, camomile, verveine, rosehip, and countless other plants are employed and enjoyed as "tea." To avoid confusion, it is better to use the term *tisane* for any drinks made from flowers, barks, roots, or leaves that do not come from the tea plant, *Camellia sinensis*. Herbals have their place and give their pleasures too, but one does not need to swear allegiance to the tea plant alone, in aroma, to see the wisdom of calling things by their names. If it doesn't come from the tea plant, it should not be called "tea," especially when the French have the right word for it— *tisane*. Derived from the Greek, this is a term that tea lovers have long preferred and that is gradually winning public acceptance.

Chai (rhymes with pie)

Chai is America's hot new drink. Coffee-houses are racking up sales serving this beverage, hot and cold. Either way, it's delicious; but I needed some tutoring, so I turned to my dear friend, Dr. Anil Sanghera, a native of India who resides and practices medicine in Baltimore, Maryland.

Anil supplies us with the following delightful description of Chai . . .

Chai is far beyond the rudiments of a simple cup of tea; any time in India is Chai time. It is served as the last course of elaborately planned feasts and offered to a beggar as a substitute for a meal. Chai, with a touch of gossip, is gleefully savored many times a day in the drawing rooms of the wealthy and enjoyed with loud slurps by the homeless on the roadsides.

The flavor of Chai can vary regionally, even from one household to another, but the basic recipe for Chai is amazingly unaltered and is as diverse as India. In Punjabi, a northern state adjacent to the national capital, New Delhi, Chai is frequently called Chaah, *the "ah" pronounced the traditional American way. Chaah is also an abbreviation of the Urdu word* Chaahat, *which means "to desire." The Punjabis truly love their Chaah.*

At the truck stops along the highways, Chai is requested by speed. The high-speed Chai tastes strong, looks dark, and gives a higher caffeine kick. A sixty-mile Chai usually has double of all ingredients and is boiled for ten to fifteen minutes. But a 100 m.p.h. Chai is left on low heat for hours and is guaranteed to wake you up and curl your tongue. The vendors on the railway platforms all over India, hawk "paan, bidi, and Chai" in the same tune like a national anthem (beetlenut leaf concoctions, cigarettes, and Chai).

A fragrant aroma, an amalgamation of many spices, this beverage, hot or cold, will seduce you. Cardamom, cloves, and cinnamon are Anil's choices for Chai, but you can also add ginger and fennel seeds. Any and all of the above listed spices may be used, but three is the optimal choice. Seeds from one cardamom pod with a pinch of ground cinnamon are used commonly. Anil's recipe is on page 152.

Tiazzi (pronounced tee-aht-see)

Tiazzi is Starbuck's new tea-based frozen fruit drink, which comes in Mango Citrus or Wild Berry.

How to Store Tea

Tea needs to be kept dry. Humidity is the number one enemy of tea. Use special tin cans, containers with lids, or a light-proof glass bottle with a tight cover.

- Store tea in a cool, dark place away from heat and sunlight.
- Store tea in small amounts.
- Green tea stored in a refrigerator needs to be sealed in an airless plastic bag and put in a tea can.

Chapter Ten

Favorite Recipes

Smoked Chicken with Apricot, Grapes, and Parmesan Cracker Tea Sandwiches

Ingredients:

Spread:

1 whole smoked chicken breast, cubed

1 tablespoon whole-grain mustard

$^1/_4$ cup mayonnaise

Salt to taste

White pepper to taste

Directions:

Purée the above ingredients until smooth and spreadable.

Other ingredients:

White bread (crust removed and cut to 3 x 1$^1/_2$-inch size)

Parmesan crackers (Spread Parmesan cheese on the bottom of a well-oiled cookie sheet. Bake at 300 degrees until crisp. Break into small pieces.)

Red grapes, halved

Apricot wedges, quartered

Directions:

1. Spread chicken mixture lightly on bread.

2. Place apricot wedges at bottom.

3. Place grape half at top, cut side down.

4. Stick Parmesan cracker in center for height.

5. Garnish with chervil or parsley.

—The Ritz-Carlton,
Tysons Corner, Virginia

Benedictine
Tea Sandwiches

Miss Jennie Benedict, a well-known Louisville,
Kentucky, caterer, is credited with creating
this classic sandwich spread at the turn of
the century.

Ingredients:

12 ounces cream cheese, softened to room temperature	Mayonnaise
	Salt to taste
1 small onion, grated	1 pound wheat bread, crust removed and cut out like diamonds
2 medium cucumbers, peeled and seeded	

Directions:

1. Grate cucumbers and combine with cream cheese.
2. Blend in onion and salt to taste.
3. Stir in a little mayonnaise just to make the mixture spreadable.
4. Spread the mixture evenly over pieces of bread that have been cut out with a cookie cutter.
5. Garnish with a thin slide of cucumber or parsley. *Makes about 45 small open-faced sandwiches.*

— *Excerpted with permission from*
A Year of Teas at the Elmwood Inn
by Shelley and Bruce Richardson, 1994.

Hummus with Alfalfa, Tomato, and Cucumber Tea Sandwiches

Ingredients:

1 15¹/₂-ounce can garbanzos beans, drained

1 garlic clove, crushed

1 tablespoon tahini

1 tablespoon olive oil

Salt to taste

White pepper to taste

Juice of 1 lemon

Directions:

Purée the above ingredients until smooth
and spreadable.

Other ingredients:

Pumpernickel bread (trimmed and cut to
   3 x 1¹/₂-inch size)

Alfalfa sprouts

Roma tomatoes (quartered and sliced very thin)

English cucumber (quartered and sliced very thin)

Directions:

1. Spread hummus very lightly on bread. Place small
   pinch of sprouts in center.
2. Place 2 pieces each of cucumber and tomato
   on opposite ends.

— The Ritz-Carlton,
Tysons Corner, Virginia

Blood Orange and Asparagus Tea Sandwiches

Ingredients:

15$\frac{1}{2}$-ounce container ricotta cheese

Juice and zest of 2 blood oranges

Pencil-size asparagus tips

Blood orange slices, cut into small wedges

White bread (crust removed and cut to
   3 x 1$\frac{1}{2}$-inch size)

Directions:

1. Mix cheese and blood orange juice together until creamy. Fold in zest.
2. Spread cheese mixture lightly on bread.
3. Place 1 wedge of blood orange at bottom of sandwich.
4. Fan 3 small asparagus spears above

*— The Ritz-Carlton,
Tysons Corner, Virginia*

Cheese Biscuits

Ingredients:

1/2 cup (1 stick) butter (no substitutes)

1/2 pound sharp Cheddar cheese, grated

2 cups unbleached all-purpose flour

1/2 teaspoon salt

Cayenne pepper to taste

2 tablespoons buttermilk

Directions:

1. Preheat the oven to 350 degrees.

2. Cream the butter and cheese together in a large bowl. In a separate bowl, combine the flour, salt, and cayenne pepper and mix well.

3. Spoon the flour mixture into the butter and cheese mixture 1 tablespoon at a time, mixing well after each addition. Add the buttermilk and mix well.

4. Roll out the dough on a floured surface and cut with a small cutter (the size of a quarter or half-dollar coin). Prick each round with a fork.

5. Place on an ungreased baking sheet and bake until lightly browned, 10–12 minutes.

To serve:

Split cheese biscuits and spread with a small amount of orange marmalade. Replace tops and heat to serve warm, or serve at room temperature. Cheese biscuits may also be served plain as a savory, along with tea sandwiches.

— *Kay Snipes and Terri Eager,*
Magnolia & Ivy Tea Rooms
Plains, Georgia

Classic Scones

Ingredients:

5 cups all-purpose flour

1 cup softened butter

2 cups whole milk

3 eggs

3 tablespoons baking powder

2 cups raisins (or currants)

Directions:

1. Mix flour and baking powder.

2. Add butter and mix until mixture crumbles.

3. Add milk and eggs and mix until
   a dough forms.

4. Fold in raisins.

5. Roll dough to 1¼ inches thick.

6. Cut out with a round cutter and
   place on a baking sheet.

7. Let scones chill in refrigerator for 30 minutes.

8. Egg wash the top of the scones and bake at
   325 degrees for 25 minutes.

9. Serve warm with preserves and
   Devonshire cream.

— The Ritz-Carlton,
Tysons Corner, Virginia

Elmwood Devonshire Cream

Our version of this English tea classic is made
with a sour cream base. Serve with scones.

Ingredients:

1 cup heavy whipping cream

½ cup powdered sugar

1½ teaspoons white vanilla extract

1 8-ounce carton sour cream

Directions:

1. Beat whipping cream, sugar, and vanilla
   until stiff.
2. Fold sour cream into this mixture
   and refrigerate. Serve with warm scones.

Excerpted with permission from
A Year of Teas at the Elmwood Inn
by Shelley and Bruce Richardson, 1994.

Blueberry Bars

Crust ingredients:

1 cup flour

$^1/_2$ cup butter, softened

$^1/_2$ cup confectioners' sugar

Directions:

Preheat oven to 350 degrees. Blend all ingredients and press into an 8- or 9-inch square pan. Bake for 15 minutes or until edges are just beginning to turn golden.

Filling ingredients:

1 cup sour cream

1 egg, beaten

1 cup sugar

1 teaspoon vanilla

$^1/_2$ teaspoon almond extract

$^1/_4$ teaspoon salt

2 tablespoons flour

2 cups fresh blueberries

Directions:

Combine sour cream, egg, sugar, vanilla, almond extract, salt and flour. Beat until smooth. Fold in blueberries. Pour into shell and bake at 400 degrees for 25 minutes.

Topping ingredients:

3 tablespoons butter, softened

3 tablespoons flour

3 tablespoons sugar

$1/4$ cup sliced almonds

Directions:

Combine all ingredients. Sprinkle over pie and bake 10 additional minutes. Chill before serving.

Excerpted with permission from
A Tea for All Seasons
by Shelley and Bruce Richardson
(Crescent Hill Books, 1996).

Irish Lace Cookies

The texture of these elegant cookies will remind you of fine Irish lace. They may be made ahead of time and stored in an airtight container.

Ingredients:

1 cup unsalted butter

$^1/_2$ cup all-purpose flour

2 cups firmly packed brown sugar

2 tablespoons vanilla

$^1/_4$ cup milk

2 cups old-fashioned rolled oats

Directions:

1. Preheat oven to 350 degrees.
2. Grease and flour two baking sheets.
3. Cream butter and sugar.
4. Add vanilla; stir in flour, milk, and rolled oats.
5. Drop batter by the tablespoon onto prepared baking sheets; allow room for cookies to spread to about 3 inches in diameter. Each baking sheet will hold about 6 cookies.

Excerpted with permission from
The Great Tea Rooms of Britain
*by Bruce Richardson
(Crescent Hill Books, 1997).*

Maypole Cake

Swirls of red raspberries discovered in each slice of this delicious cake will remind you of long streamers flowing down from a maypole. You may feel like a child again!

Ingredients:

2 sticks butter, softened	1/2 teaspoon salt
3 cups sugar	1 teaspoon vanilla
6 eggs	1/2 teaspoon lemon flavoring
3 cups all-purpose flour	1/4 teaspoon orange flavoring
1 cup sour cream	1/4 teaspoon almond flavoring
1/4 teaspoon soda	1/4 cup raspberry preserves

Directions:

1. Cream butter and sugar; add eggs, one at a time.
2. Add flour alternately with sour cream, beating after each addition.
3. Add soda and salt; beat well and add flavorings.
4. Preheat oven to 325 degrees.
5. Pour one-half of batter into a greased tube pan.
6. Warm preserves enough to spread evenly over batter.
7. Add remaining batter. Swirl a knife through the batter a couple of times in order to gently cut in the layer of preserves.
8. Bake for 70–80 minutes.

Excerpted with permission from
A Year of Teas at the Elmwood Inn
by Shelley and Bruce Richardson, 1994.

Chai

To serve two cups of Chai

Ingredients:

2 teaspoons loose tea

2 teaspoons sugar

2 cups water

1/2 cup whole milk

2 cloves

1/4 inch piece of cinnamon

10–15 seeds from 1 green cardamom pod
   (Discard the pod or outer green shell.)

Directions:

1. Add the water to a saucepan and
   bring to a boil.

2. Allow to boil for 30 seconds.

3. Add the tea, cloves, cinnamon, and cardamom
   seeds to the boiling water, cover
   the saucepan, and remove from heat.

4. Allow to steep for 5 minutes.

5. Return to heat and add the milk.

6. Bring to a gentle boil uncovered and
   remove from heat.

7. Allow to sit for 2 minutes, strain, and serve.

Note:

To bring out a stronger taste of spices, use a little extra water and boil for 1 minute. You can also let it sit longer after adding tea leaves, but make sure to reduce the amount to 1¹/₂ teaspoons. Letting the mixture sit longer after adding milk also allows the spices and tea to reach an optimal level.

— Dr. Anil Sanghera

Index

Notes